A Guide to Effective Internal Management System Audits

Implementing internal audits as a risk management tool

A Guide to Effective Internal Management System Audits

Implementing internal audits
as a risk management tool

ANDREW W. NICHOLS

IT Governance Publishing

IT Governance Publishing
IT Governance Limited
Unit 3, Clive Court
Bartholomew's Walk
Cambridgeshire Business Park
Ely, Cambridgeshire
CB7 4EA
United Kingdom
www.itgovernance.co.uk

© Andrew W. Nichols 2014

The author has asserted the rights of the author under the Copyright, Designs and Patents Act, 1988, to be identified as the author of this work.

First published in the United Kingdom in 2014
by IT Governance Publishing.

ISBN 978-1-84928-559-9

FOREWORD

The word "audit" comes from the Latin audītus meaning the act of hearing. A benign definition, so it's strange then, that the idea of an audit is often viewed negatively by people. Typically, this comes from the spectre of an income tax audit or those performed by a regulatory agency, which is common in the food, pharmaceutical, and health and safety industries.

Since the early 1960s, it has become more and more common for purchasers to audit their supply chain, sometimes with terrible results! For example, the UK's Ministry of Defence had ordered a maritime attack and patrol aircraft from the supplier BAE, known as the "Nimrod MRA4." Development started in 1996 and in 2010, the project was canceled at which point it was £789 million over budget and more than nine years late. The UK newspaper, the Financial Times, reported (in January 2011):

> "Safety tests conducted [in 2010] found there were still 'several hundred design non-compliances' with the aircraft. It was unclear, for example, whether its bomb bay doors functioned properly, whether its landing gear worked and, most worryingly, whether its fuel pipe was safe."

At no point did any of the auditors, who were evaluating the various subcontractors, formally report that any problems were being encountered!

Since the early 1990s, a number of international standards have been published that define requirements for management systems, including ISO9001 for the quality management of products, ISO14001 for environmental controls, ISO/TS 16949 for automotive product suppliers, ISO13485 for medical device manufacturers, and, more recently, ISO20000 for information services and ISO27001 for information security.

The requirements specified in each of the preceding standards describe many topics that are common with – and based on – ISO9001, specifically those that relate to:

- management review
- corrective action
- preventive action
- document and records control
- internal audits
- improvement

In most cases, the requirement for implementing management system internal audits is practically identical to that found in ISO9001.

Originally, ISO9001 (and its precursor, British Standard BS5750) was created to be the basis for agreement on how (product) quality would be systematically assured between customer and supplier organizations. At about the same time in the UK, the use of so-called "Third Party Certification" became an option for purchasing organizations (typically the UK government-owned utilities and other agencies like the Ministries of Defence, Public Buildings and Works etc.) to use, in place of their own supplier evaluations.

The third-party certification bodies (or "registrars" in the US), as they have become known, audited subscribing organizations for compliance to the ISO9001 requirements. At about the same time, training organizations started offering training courses for people to learn how to perform internal management systems audits. Furthermore, another auditor training course also became popular, the so-called "lead auditor" course. Based on supplier Quality Assurance auditing techniques, this became the de facto training for certification body auditors, since it formed part of the accreditation criteria developed by the International Register of Certificate Auditors (IRCA). Auditor course accreditation became important in establishing credibility.

The lead auditor course, usually of 36 h duration, has become very popular over the past two decades, since it is often perceived as being a way to experience and learn how a certification body auditor will perform a certification audit. Attendees are, in many cases, those responsible for leading the implementation of a Quality Management System to meet ISO9001 to achieve certification or who have been identified as the internal auditor.

Internal auditor training courses usually cover the basic audit technical content of the Lead Auditor course, but in a reduced format, over a 16 or 24-h duration.

Although thousands of people have been trained through attendance at this type of course, what isn't well understood is that the style of auditing experienced by the attendees is based on external audit principles and techniques, which focus almost exclusively on compliance to the ISO requirements. Many organizations have no benchmark for how internal audits really should be performed and those who experience customers' quality audits recognize a good deal of similarity.

Unfortunately, much of the training content doesn't fully address the needs of the organization's audit program with the result that rarely are the true benefits of effectively managed internal audits fully realized.

This book gives guidance and a model for the management and implementation of internal audits, which moves beyond simple compliance to ISO requirements, dispenses with the typical external audit-based practices – which may be perceived as offering more "style than substance" – and becomes a transformational tool that the organization can use to assist with the management of risk.

PREFACE

There is a lot of misunderstanding about the role of internal audits in the implementation of a management system. The range of expectations of internal audits ranges from confirming simple compliance of activities compared with documentation at one end of the scale, to that of identifying improvements at the opposite end.

Furthermore, it is commonly expressed that auditors should be somewhat god-like in their knowledge and understanding of many facets of auditing. Yet, oddly, audit programs are rarely given much top-management support in key areas:

- audit planning
- auditor selection/competency
- post-audit actions

In many cases, internal management systems audits are new to organizations. Certainly, they may have had some experience of audits but, for the most part, these audits are performed by outsiders to the organization and, hence, considered "external audits." It isn't entirely clear how internal audits are supposed to work for the organization's management and the employees. Much of the currently available training is predominantly based on a model developed for external (supplier quality, financial, or regulatory) auditors – the accredited "ISO9000 lead auditor" course is a classic example (more of which later).

So, how can the role of internal audits become better understood by the organization's management (and others)?

Let's draw an analogy to explain the role of the internal auditor:

The design and implementation of a management system is somewhat similar to the design and production of a (new) product, which may be depicted as this simple diagram:

There are key inputs to the design process:

- customer
- regulatory/statutory
- organizational

The output from the design process is documented in a manner that can be used to make the product. This documentation is, or rather should be, developed in conjunction with those who have to make and test the product. The documentation is often in the form of instructions, process control requirements, critical features for inspection and so on, and what is followed to ensure the process meets the intended specifications.

Once the product is made, it is passed over for inspection and test. This confirms, independently, that the design specifications have been met by the processes which made the product. If it doesn't meet the specifications, the reasons are recorded and it is decided – by those who have authority, often in conjunction with the design "owner" – what can be done to correct it (repair, rework, replacement etc).

In a similar manner, the "design" of the management system, the resulting processes, and controls are created, with customer, regulatory, and the organization's interests being considered. These various requirements are implemented throughout the organization. The implementation can be independently verified as being "to the specification" in a similar manner as a product is inspected and tested. Indeed, an audit is often considered in some business sectors as a "test" of the organization.

It follows then, that any discrepancies of the implemented management system will be brought to the appropriate people for action.

ABOUT THE AUTHOR

Andrew (Andy) W. Nichols has more than 25 years of experience of management systems and auditing. His wide-ranging experience of management systems standards includes NATO "AQAP 1," BS5750, ISO9001, QS-9000, ISO14001, ISO/TS 16949, and ISO/IEC 17025.

In 1985, Andy became the first internal Quality Systems Internal Auditor for a major metrology equipment manufacturer and, as its Supplier Quality Manager attended one of the very first Lead Auditor of quality management systems training courses. He then joined the first UK accredited management systems certification body (LRQA) as a Lead Auditor, quickly becoming a supervisor and trainer, responsible for mentoring new certification auditors. During this time, he performed one of the first ISO9000 Certification audits in the US.

In 1992, he pursued a career as a consultant and trainer with Excel Partnership Inc., a leading provider of ISO-based management systems implementation support. In this role he has delivered hundreds of ISO9000-related training courses, specializing in Internal and Lead Auditor training.

As an instructional designer, Andy led, and contributed to, the development of "best in class" management systems internal and lead auditor training courses for ISO9001, ISO14001, ISO/IEC 17024, QS-9000, ISO/TS 16949, and ISO/IEC 17025. This wide-ranging experience of management systems audits in all roles (first, second, and third party) gives Andy a unique perspective on the purposes, tools, techniques, and practices. He has developed a unique planning tool, the "Football" diagram, for planning a process-based audit.

His clients have included Tellabs, Chrysler, GKN, General Motors, Visteon, Hyundai Motor Manufacturing of America, Hewlett-Packard, Dresser Industries, ANSI, the USDA, and many branches of the US Department of Defense.

During his career, Andy has held Certifications with the International Register of Certificated Auditors (IRCA) and the RABQSA organization as a Lead Auditor of quality management systems. He has been a corporate member of the UK's Chartered Institute of Quality and a member of the American Society for Quality (ASQ) since 1986.

He has been employed by the global certification body NQA, USA as its East Coast Sales Manager since early 2008. Bringing more than 25 years' experience to the role, he has contributed to NQA's overall sales success. Andy is also author of the implementation guide, "Exploding the Myths Surrounding ISO9001[1]."

A regular technical contributor to the largest Internet forum for management systems, known as the "Elsmar Cove" (*www.elsmar.com/forums*), where he is also a forum moderator, Andy can be found on the social media networking site LinkedIn, (*www.linkedin.com/pub/andy-nichols/6/728/173*), where he is an active member of many groups and owner of the "Quality Management Discussions" group.

Andy currently lives in Michigan with his Golden Retriever, "Winston."

---

[1] *www.itgovernance.co.uk/shop/p-1292-exploding-the-myths-surrounding-iso9000-a-practical-implementation-guide.aspx.*

ACKNOWLEDGEMENTS

I extend my sincere appreciation to the following people:

Jeff Monk – trained me as an internal management system auditor and then as a management system "lead auditor." Jeff wrote one of the very first recognized lead auditor courses.

David Middleton – for giving me the opportunity to pursue a career as a trainer and consultant with Excel Partnership Inc., and the countless clients I had the privilege of training as auditors.

John Owen, IAF Secretariat – for permission to reproduce various IAF documents.

Dr David Stoddart, who was the Quality Manager at Renishaw Metrology Ltd., and gave me my first opportunity to be trained and pursue a career as a management system "lead auditor."

The many clients and their management systems I have been allowed to audit.

The many professionals I've met during the course of my career, for providing me with the opportunities to see their challenges with implementing management system internal audits and using that to develop the understanding contained in this book.

My thanks also to Donald Lessels, Senior Management Systems Lead Assessor, LRQA and Marc Taillefer, IT Service Management technical expert, consultant, trainer and coach, for their helpful contributions during the review process.

Acknowledgements

ISO 9000 is adopted by national standards bodies around the world. Where we refer to or quote specific text within the Standard, we are referring to the original ISO version. Readers of this book should purchase their own copy of this international Standard.

CONTENTS

INTRODUCTION

Internal audits are required to be performed by any organization wishing to comply with any of the international standards for management systems, for example ISO9001, ISO14001, ISO13485, ISO27001 and so on. Although certification of organizations to these management systems standards has been available for nearly 25 years, the requirements were written to be implemented without the need for external certification audits. If internal audits are not used to "prepare" an organization for the audits of a Certification Body, why are they (universally) required by these standards?

Today, most organizations wishing to implement an ISO standards-based management system often utilize available (often accredited) training for management systems auditors. This training is, for the most part, frequently based upon the model for external (supplier) audits. Furthermore, the requirements set down by accreditation bodies for auditor courses and, therefore, course providers, make little distinction between the needs of internal versus external audits and auditors. The word "internal" is often overlooked in many aspects of the world of auditor training, audit program implementation, consulting, and performing internal audits. That is to say "internal" in terms of the needs of those inside the organization, behaviors, culture, needs, and expectations.

Those organizations seeking a third-party certification of their management system may send their auditor candidates to training courses that proceed to demonstrate the external audit model. In the early stages of implementation, the focus is on compliance with the ISO standards and movement toward certification. The use of the external audit model is subsequently recognized by the certification body auditor who may have attended a similar training course. The internal audit program often replicates the third-party audits, even leading to a successful certification (also known as registration). Furthermore, the typical people involved in management systems audits are often those who are employed in the Quality function and for whom the conventions of audits are often most associated with regulatory, customer, and/or supplier focused.

Even years after certification is achieved, the internal audit program may fail to develop beyond maintaining simple compliance. In short, the audits that are performed can sit like a "square peg in a round hole" of the management system.

This book provides guidance describing how an organization may develop key features of its internal audits beyond the external audit model and toward true internal audits, by using an approach based on risk management.

CHAPTER 1: MANAGEMENT SYSTEMS AUDITS – A BACKGROUND

Auditing of organizations has been a regular occurrence in various industries for many years. Before the advent of the most commonly known international standards for management systems, major procurement organizations and regulatory agencies were auditing throughout the supply chain as a means to evaluate those suppliers involved.

For the purposes of this guide, it is worth beginning by defining what an audit is, in the context of a management system requirement such as ISO9001, ISO14001 and so on. In some industries, the term audit and inspection (Quality control activities) are used interchangeably.

In the context of a management system internal audit, the following definition is applicable:

"Systematic, independent and documented process for obtaining audit evidence and evaluating it objectively to determine the extent to which audit criteria are fulfilled".

ISO19011:2011, 3.1

Note:

Other common types of audit may be associated within the context of a management system and should not be confused with the subject of this guide:

- Control Plan (Process) Audits
- Product Audits
- Layered Process Audits

Control plan (process) audits are common in, for example, the automotive manufacturing supply chain and are usually an audit of the manufacturing line, evaluated against the "process control plan." In the food industry the audit is carried out against an H.A.C.C.P (hazard analysis and critical control points) plan.

Product audits are also common in a variety of industries: automotive, food processing, and pharmaceuticals. These audits are carried out usually on finished, packed product against the relevant product-related specifications.

Layered Process Audits is an audit method mainly required by top-tier customers of their lower-level suppliers in the automotive supply chain, to determine if their suppliers' process controls are in place on the product manufacturing line and that they are working effectively. Typically, the "layers" relate to the various levels (or layers) of management involved in performing the audits.

Using a predetermined checklist, an audit of the process controls and other requirements, such as training, maintenance/calibration and so on, is performed by the line/area supervisor, on each shift running. Any issues are noted in an audit log and brought to the attention of the relevant department for action. The next layer of management/supervision then performs a similar audit, usually at a lesser frequency (weekly) and includes a review of the status of any actionable items from the first layer of audits. As each successive layer of management undertakes their audit (once again, at a reduced frequency), the focus becomes more on the actions to ensure they are, effectively, escalated to the level of management that can direct resources/budget and so on.

Apart from some very basic instructions, no training of auditors is required and, for other reasons, these layered process audits should not be considered as a replacement for the management systems audits required by the applicable ISO Standard, or "Technical Specification" (such as ISO/TS 16949).

The requirement for internal management systems audits has been present in ISO9001 and its predecessor BS5750 since their publication in 1987. The arrival of third-party certification of organizations to the ISO Standard wasn't until 1989–1990, so we can safely conclude that the reason for including internal audits in the ISO9001 Standard wasn't much to do with preparing for certification.

So why then, would the ISO9000 technical committee, TC176, responsible for authoring the Standard, have included this requirement?

Just as with other types of audits they are mainly used (by or on behalf of stakeholders) as an independent verification of the conditions prevailing (sometimes historic) at the time they are performed. They should be an evaluation of facts of whatever the objective(s) of the management system is, be it financial, regulatory, supply chain, or something else.

ISO9001, 8.2.2 states:

> *The organization shall conduct internal audits at planned intervals to determine whether the quality management system*
>
> *a) conforms to the planned arrangements (see 7.1), to the requirements of this International Standard and to the quality management system requirements established by the organization, and*
> *b) is effectively implemented.*

An audit programme shall be planned, taking into consideration the status and importance of the processes and areas to be audited, as well as the results of previous audits. The audit criteria, scope, frequency and methods shall be defined. The selection of auditors and conduct of audits shall ensure objectivity and impartiality of the audit process. Auditors shall not audit their own work.

A documented procedure shall be established to define the responsibilities and requirements for planning and conducting audits, establishing records and reporting results.

Records of audits and their results shall be maintained (see 4.2.4).

The management responsible for the area being audited shall ensure that any corrections and corrective actions are taken without undue delay to eliminate detected nonconformities and their causes.

Follow-up activities shall include verification of the actions taken and the reporting of verification results (see 8.5.2).

By further analyzing how internal audits were intended to be applied to the management system, we can better understand their role and the service that should be provided to management – as a risk-management tool.

Audits are frequently performed upon an organization by representatives of customers, government agencies, and other external bodies – now including the third-party certifiers or registrars. The predominant model of how audits are performed is, therefore, based on the activities and behaviors of those from outside the organization. They are, almost universally, external audits.

Supplier Audits

Much of the background to management systems auditing has come from the practices of major procurement organizations in those industries where supplier audits are common. These include, for example:

- medical device
- defense
- automotive
- aerospace

Often, these audits were subsequently flowed down through the supply chain to lower-tier organizations.

There are basically two fundamental reasons for performing supplier management system audits:

- supplier selection
- supplier monitoring

Each has a somewhat different focus and may be performed by a variety of personnel from the procuring organization.

Supplier Selection Audits

When an organization seeks a new supplier it is often important to gather information about that supplier and its capabilities. While it is common to send detailed questionnaires to a supplier, these cannot represent its capabilities as effectively as actually visiting its facilities and seeing, first hand, its operations. Frequently, an evaluation of the supplier's financial status is also undertaken, through a "Dunn and Bradstreet" report, or similar. The purpose of such an audit is to determine the risks associated with doing business with a supplier.

For example, the audit might focus on the potential supplier and what controls it has over its suppliers (perhaps raw materials), knows how to ensure incoming product is correct, and, therefore, protects the customer from non-conforming product. If the audit reveals the nature and effectiveness of the supplier's supplier controls, the risks to the customer can be identified and a business decision made to work with the supplier – or abandon it.

The basis of supplier "Quality Assurance" was (originally) the purpose behind the use of ISO9001 and its predecessors, BS5750, NATO AQAP 1, and so on. These standards may be applied to the whole supplier organization, but often as not, the purchasing organization's primary interest is in those aspects of the supplier's arrangements for controlling the product to be purchased and, hence, understanding the risk in using that supplier.

Where a supplier organization is found to be adequate it is common to use contractually binding QA arrangements, such as Quality Plans or Control Plans that define the agreed upon activities to ensure a quality product is the result.

In regulated industries, such as those producing medical devices, to allow those products into the marketplace, the regulatory authorities make it a requirement to define the controls needed to assure the development and production to the approved specification(s). In the US this is (in part) known as the Federal Drug Administration's "510(K)." Since the effects of making non-conforming products – drugs, pharmaceuticals and so on, or those involved in food production – can have serious and widespread consequences, the organizations throughout the supply chains involved are regularly audited to ensure conformity to the various regulations, with the intention of minimizing risk.

Supplier Monitoring Audits

Having established that a supplier organization is capable of meeting the procurement organization's needs, periodic audits may be carried out to ensure the controls put into place are still followed. These may be performed to a schedule – perhaps annually, or timed to coincide with key events in production, such as start-up, changes in facilities, specifications, facilities, and so on. Once again, the main theme of these audits will be the product-specific quality assurance arrangements.

Furthermore, should a supplier deliver suspect or non-conforming product an audit may be initiated at the supplier's site, focusing on the corrective actions taken to control and remediate the issue from reaching the customer.

Third-party Certification Audits

Originally being intended to reduce the need for multiple purchasing organization audits of suppliers, independent "third-party" certification is used to provide evidence of basic quality assurance being in place at the organization. When an organization is certified as complying with one or more international management systems standards by an accredited certification body, a purchasing organization may accept that supplier development will be minimal. Purchasing organizations may elect to augment this "ISO" certification with their own audits, as described previously, to fully understand the degree to which the supplying organization may suit their needs.

Third-party certification is described in chapter 4.

CHAPTER 2: THE ROLE OF ISO19011

In 1991, three years after ISO9001 was published, a guidance document was released by the International Standards Organization on the subject of quality management systems auditing, ISO10011. This was subsequently withdrawn and replaced, in 2002, by ISO19011, "Guidelines for quality and/or environmental management systems auditing."

The current version of ISO19011 has been tailored to be more suitable for internal audits of management systems since the arrival of ISO/IEC 17021 – "Conformity assessment – Requirements for bodies providing audit and certification of management systems" – has reduced the need for all three basic types of audit (internal, supply chain, and certification body) to be included in the one document. Interestingly, perhaps, the 2002 version of ISO19011 was, later augmented in the US (under ANSI/ISO/ASQ QE 19011S-2004) and further guidance was given specifically for the internal audit program as well as for second-party audits.

The differences between 2002 and 2011 editions are defined in the foreword as follows:

- The scope has been broadened from auditing of quality and environmental systems to the auditing of any management system.
- The relationship between ISO19011 and ISO/IEC 17021 has been clarified.
- Remote audit methods and the concept of risk have been introduced.

- Confidentiality has been added as a new principle of auditing.
- Clauses 5, 6 and 7 have been reorganized.
- Additional information has been included in a new Annex B, resulting in the removal of help boxes.
- The competence determination and evaluation has been strengthened.
- Illustrative examples of discipline specific knowledge and skills have been added in a new Annex A.
- Additional guidelines are available at the following website *www.iso.org/19011auditing.*

The document gives guidance on the following major topics:

- Terms and definitions
- Principles of auditing
- Managing an audit program
- Performing an Audit
- Competence and evaluation of Auditors

Definitions

For the purposes of discussion, throughout this book the definitions found in ISO19011:2011 and ISO9000:2005 will be used for consistency. Throughout this book, the following definitions will be referenced:

Audit

Systematic, independent, and documented process for obtaining audit evidence and evaluating it objectively to determine the extent to which audit criteria are fulfilled.

Audit criteria

Set of policies, procedures, or requirements used as a reference against which audit evidence is compared.

Audit program

Arrangements for a set of one or more audits planned for a specific time-frame and directed toward a specific purpose.

Audit plan

Description of the activity and arrangements for an audit.

ISO19011:2011 further describes the importance of risk, when managing an internal audit program:

This international standard introduces the concept of risk to management systems auditing. The approach adopted relates both to the risk of the audit process not achieving its objectives and to the potential of the audit to interfere with the auditee's activities and processes. It does not provide specific guidance on the organization's risk management process, but recognizes that organizations can focus audit effort on matters of significance to the management system."

Since ISO19011:2011 does not give this guidance, the following chapters give a practical-based approach to the development of internal audits that effectively addresses risks to the organization and its management system(s).

CHAPTER 3: THE INTERNAL AUDIT PROCESS

The requirements for internal management systems audits specified in a number of ISO standards are based heavily on those originally contained in ISO9001. A review of standards as diverse as ISO13485 for medical device manufacturers Quality Management System, and ISO/IEC 17025 for testing/calibration laboratories, to ISO22301 for Business Continuity Management, shows that the requirements for internal audits are substantially similar to the basics in ISO9001, 8.2.2.

Internal audits may be effectively managed as a process according to Dr. Shewhart's "Plan, Do, Check, Act" cycle. A diagram of the process might look like this:

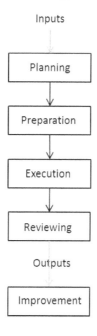

Audit Programs

In the early period of the implementation of a management system, the internal audit program is frequently established with the primary goal of preparing for a third-party certification audit. The "risk" is not attaining certification, because major non-conformities were discovered during the certification audit.

As defined earlier, an audit program is defined as one or a number of audits and, when beginning the implementation of an audit, it can be a challenge to know where to direct the audits of the fledgling management system. It may help to understand that as the system implementation evolves and matures, so the internal audit program's focus goes through three key phases (Figure 1).

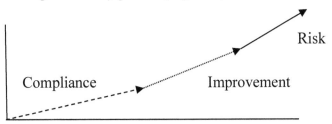

Figure 1. Audit program maturity.

Often, in the early phases of system implementation, the focus of the internal audit program is to ensure no significant issues are found during the Certification Body audit. The internal audits typically use the ISO Standard(s) as their criteria as well as determining compliance to the organization's own management system documentation and so on. This focus can be of assistance to the organization as the audits tend to be performed in a manner similar to the Certification Body audits – particularly when implemented by a person from outside the organization, such as a consultant. Experience shows that the majority of internal audits remain at this level of deployment that, while minimally maintaining compliance – and hence the required certification – often leads, inevitably, to "humdrum" and predictable audits which rarely reveal any real value to the management and the rest of the organization.

Once found in compliance, the internal audits should then be scheduled to ensure their focus changes to give value to the organization, rather than only compliance to the ISO Standard. To do this, the scheduling of audits must be changed from a "push" system, where audits are scheduled to an annual "calendar," to one of a "pull" or demand system, where they are scheduled according to management's and the other needs of the organization.

To bring the maximum benefit to the organization, internal management systems audits must be elevated to a role where they are used to evaluate "risk." The international Standard on risk management, ISO31000, defines risk as:

"An undesirable situation or circumstance that has both a likelihood of occurring and a potentially negative consequence" or the "effect of uncertainty on objectives."

It follows, therefore, that the internal audits should be employed to evaluate the management system under conditions that may have an effect on its ability to assure control.

One challenge for those who wish to elevate their internal audits along the maturity curve from compliance to risk, may struggle to find any indications within the requirements to assist them. In fact, the requirements are there, but hidden!

The ISO9001 requirements for internal audits (8.2.2) give us a clue what might be considered when establishing an audit schedule (also called an audit program). It states (in part):

"An audit program shall be established taking into consideration the status and importance of the processes to be audited."

This requirement provides us some opportunities to consider that all processes are not created equally, that some might need to be audited as a priority and possibly more frequently than others. So, how can an audit program meet these requirements and be value added to an organization in tackling risk?

Let's consider what's meant by the "status" of the processes of the Quality Management System:

Status might include something being new and/or changed, performing below or above expectations. Experience tells us that having something new or changed associated with the following list is frequently associated with being problematic:

- customers and requirements
- suppliers
- technology
- regulations
- process requirements
- materials, equipment and so on

These may also be considered to be risks to the business: how many of us have heard there's a risk in buying a new model car or other product until after it's been on the market for a year – until there's been time to "work the problems out"? What would be the risk to the business of a loss of customer satisfaction, or a major recall?

Likewise, a process not performing to expectations, causing scrap, rework, and downtime – in fact any kind of waste – is also a risk. Got a process that exceeded its goal? Better find out why! If the bar has been raised and the customer notices, then expectations may now be set at that higher level of performance. Once the reason has been discovered, it could also be used to improve other, similar processes.

In some cases, these are planned situations – including the new and changed aspects – and others, like poor performance, are unplanned. What could be done to give a priority to an audit of a new, changed, or poorly performing process? This is where the importance of the process must be considered.

We have to ask ourselves, is the process important to meeting:

- customer needs and expectations?
- regulatory compliance?
- cost targets?

The importance of the process as seen by the customer or the effect on other aspects of business can be considered as the impact of that process on the business. Remember:

> *"An undesirable situation or circumstance that has both a likelihood of occurring and a potentially negative consequence" or the "effect of uncertainty on objectives."*

It is common for internal audit programs to be developed on an annual calendar that predicts which aspects of the

Quality Management System are going to be audited. Often the objectives for developing the schedule are to ensure all the system is audited in that year, or to ensure all the ISO requirements are covered, and so on. However, since there is no requirement to perform audits in that way, these internal audits often miss critical processes when they become an issue.

In one company, interns were recruited as seasonal workers (to cover during summer vacation time) on an assembly line, which resulted in almost predictable product quality problems. The internal audit schedule forced the auditors to focus on features of the management system that were rarely problematic – instead of taking a critical look at the training and competency of the new people.

Imagine the hapless line supervisor having to act like a "mother hen" to his or her new operators while attempting to answer auditors' questions about product labeling, document control, and so on! Had the audit schedule directed the auditors to the training process when it was being implemented, it's highly likely to have diagnosed the problem with the process and attracted management's support for corrective actions.

[Interestingly, the Certification Body auditors had apparently never made an issue of this example of lack of effectiveness, despite the fact that the performance of the company's processes was displayed on a huge report card in the lunch room!]

Audit Program Planning

In preparing for battle I have always found that plans are useless, but planning is indispensable (Dwight Eisenhower)

The requirements for internal management systems planning from the ISO standards states that, "an audit programme shall be planned..." The definition of "audit programme" from ISO19011 states that it is "one or more audits."

When implementation of a management system is initiated, the focus on internal audits is often to prepare for a Third-party Certification audit. As a consequence, it becomes desirable to be able to a) demonstrate the internal audit process is (substantially) implemented as planned and, b) to ensure the "four corners" of the management system have been covered by the internal audits with the goal of ensuring nothing has been missed, which could result in a "major" non-conformity (which would prevent registration). From these expectations, it is typical that a calendar (as shown next) is developed by the internal audit process owner because of a (perceived) need (some Certification Body contracts require this) to cover the complete management system, or requirements of the ISO Standard, in 12 months.

	J	F	M	A	M	J	J	A	S	O	N	D
4	X											
4.1		X						X				
4.2				X								
5.1					X							
5.2					X							

5.3		X	
5.4			X
5.5			X

And so on, through to the final "elements"

8.4	X
8.5	X

The use of an annualized calendar forces audits of processes that are either not a high priority (a risk) or cause the audit to occur before/after any problems transpire, instead of helping to identify what contemporary actions need to be taken. No wonder then, that in many organizations the internal audit program is not well supported! Internal audits should be scheduled using current process performance data, feedback from customers, and so on, to ensure auditors are focused on what is on management's "radar screen."

Once the management system and, hence, the internal audit program has been implemented, non-conformities may arise – either from audits performed by the internal auditors or from the Certification Body (and possibly customer auditors) – and these lead to further internal audits. Despite being labeled as "ad hoc" audits (or some such similar name), in the eyes of management, and don't follow the previously issued calendar. Such changes to a schedule may cast doubt on the ability to create a plan and stick to it!

Internal audit management programs, scheduled based on risk and impact, can help usher in a new era, synonymous with risk assessment and continual improvements, rather than something done simply for compliance. Furthermore, the role of auditor becomes elevated in status similar to that of a Six Sigma/Kaizen practitioner. Improving the internal audit program in this manner will help to ensure a domino effect on corrective actions and the management reviews of the Quality Management System as a whole.

If internal audits are considered to be a process[2] (interestingly, the ISO requirement is for a documented procedure, not a documented process), then we must consider and identify the inputs to the process. If we discount the need for Third-party Certification of Management Systems as being an input to the internal audit program, then what might be considered to be the inputs that will be factors in managing a number of internal audits?

Audit Frequency

As stated earlier, when establishing an audit program, the default activity is often to construct a calendar of audits to be carried out, often over a 12-month period. A frequency is chosen, somewhat arbitrarily, and may be based on what the person thinks they can "get to," given their other duties, and so on.

A common approach is to set a frequency of monthly, quarterly, semi-annually, or even annually. The audit events are then fitted to the calendar, often with the intent of ensuring all the requirements of the Standard or the management system are covered within a year.

---

[2] A process is defined in ISO9000 as "activities which transform inputs into outputs."

Where's the risk?

Audit programs that are simply fitted to a 12-month calendar (or similar) rarely take risk into consideration. As stated previously, they "push" an audit on some part of the organization. Since there is little or no input to the planning from the management of the organization, there may be little consideration of anything that resembles the "effect of uncertainty on objectives."

Once the internal audit program is implemented, and non-conformances are found, it is usual to factor the corrective actions into the next audits, which may be the closest to a consideration of risk.

Audit Scope

Each audit planned should have a defined scope. As the name suggests, in the same way as a telescope or microscope allows the viewer to focus in on a subject, the scope provides a focus for an auditor and helps set boundaries to be set for their audit assignment. There are benefits to a well-defined audit scope that are often overlooked:

- allows accurate planning and preparation
- assignment of qualified auditor(s) to ensure no one audits their own work
- identification of duration of audit
- establishes expectations for the auditor(s)
- provides a means of time management for the auditor

In the early period of implementation of the management system, the audit scope may be the whole system (often covered at one time) or individual process/procedures. Since compliance with the ISO requirements is a priority, in preparation for certification, the risk is simply that of failing the stage 2 audit[3] (or a subsequent surveillance audit). In many cases, this is where internal audits languish.

Where's the risk?

In order to use internal audits as an effective tool, the scope should be adjusted to consider the parts of the management system that have been associated with an identified risk. Rather than actual processes, experience shows that it's often the interface between organizations and their processes that present the highest risk.

Examples include:

• sales and manufacturing
• product development and suppliers
• product development and field service

Audit Criteria

Each audit is, in basic terms, a comparison of the degree of conformity to a specified requirement. The requirement against which the audit is conducted may be selected by management or the audit program manager. When the goal of the organization is implementing a management system in compliance to an ISO Standard's requirements, it's common to choose and to perform an audit of the organization compared to them. As we can see in both the

---

[3]See chapter on Third-party Certification for a description.

internal audit requirements and the diagram of the management system's maturity, using ISO standards as audit criteria is perfectly valid in the initial stages.

Where's the risk?

It should be noted, however, that other criteria are available and should be used. Available criteria that can and should be used by internal audits include:

- regulatory requirements
- customer requirements
- service level agreements
- management systems requirements including documents such as policies, objectives, processes, procedures, instructions, quality plans, and so on

As can be seen from this list, when combined with an audit scope statement, internal audits can be wide-ranging or, alternatively, sharply focused on a particular aspect of the organization that may present a risk to the achievement and performance to these criteria.

Once an auditor's assignment has clearly defined scope and criteria, the next activity is the auditor's individual planning and preparation.

Auditor Planning & Preparation

"Good planning and hard work lead to prosperity"
(Proverbs 21:5)

The planning and preparation activities of any audit shouldn't be overlooked or made into a cursory activity.

While it may be tempting to thrust a prepared checklist into an auditor's hand and tell them "go audit," it must be avoided if the auditor is to be effective. An individual auditor's preparation for their audit assignment is fundamental to ensuring they have "ownership" of the conduct and results of that audit ("people own what they create").

Once an audit assignment is given to an auditor, they should be focused on the processes of the Quality Management System and recurring questions auditors have included: "How do I audit a process?" "Which processes should I start with?" and "How will I know if the process is effective?"

One fundamental difference between the external auditor and the internal auditor is that the internal variety has a greater ability (and usually more time/access) to involve the management of the organization in the planning and preparation for their audit. A significant portion of the ground work necessary to answer the preceding questions can be researched by working with the person who is the owner of the process/area to be audited. It is they who have most to benefit from knowing the risks associated with their process and which part(s) of the management system contribute to the risk(s) or their mitigation. See case study #1.

Through time spent by the internal auditor in working with the process owner, more effective planning can be carried out to ensure the subsequent audit doesn't miss that which is important to the overall performance of the process. Perhaps paradoxically, the third party audit process includes this particular activity and is known as the "Stage 1" audit.

Audit Planning Tools

Performing an audit can be a complex task, when considering the audit criteria set for the auditor, with many points to consider. The purpose and benefits of an individual auditor's planning for their audit cannot be overstated since it brings many benefits to the audit program as a whole, as well as to the effectiveness of the auditor and, therefore, audit results. A variety of planning tools are available to auditors that are discussed next:

Checklists

One tool in common use, and often associated with audits, is the so-called "checklist." The use of checklists is a controversial subject in the audit "business," and even the mere name can bring people out in a rash of dislike. There is nothing inherently "wrong" with a checklist, however, some checklists are just what the name implies – a list of items, sometimes based on the audit criteria, often in the form of questions the auditor asks, to be "checked off" as each is completed. The idea that a management systems audit could be as simple as asking questions from a list and soliciting an answer that could then be checked off the list is considered controversial by some audit professionals.

Typically, those audits that are performed using the international management system standards as the audit criteria often use checklists which rephrase each section of the requirements as a question.

For example, ISO9001 states (in part) in section 6.4, "The organization shall determine and manage the work environment…" A checklist, based on this, would simply read, "Has the organization determined and managed the work environment"? Such questions usually solicit a simple "yes" or "no" answer. At worst, questions phrased using words from the Standard and directed at an organization's personnel would likely result in a quizzical look by the person being audited. At best, a simple non-conformity is likely to be recorded.

During the early stages of implementation of a management system, such a checklist can be of use in compiling "gap analysis" audit of the organization's existing practices compared to the requirements of one of the standards. Typically, they are best completed at the conclusion of the gap assessment audit, rather than being used as a tool to guide the auditor, and can provide a simple report on status compared to the Standard. However, as an internal management systems audit planning tool, they are of limited use.

It is true to say there are some basics that can form the essence of nearly all internal audits; document and record control, for example. However, the use of "canned" or predefined checklists (many are available on the Internet, for example) miss the important activity of the auditor studying for their assignment and being involved in planning.

In addition to checklists, other forms of audit planning tools have come to prominence in recent years:

Turtle Diagrams

Since the release of the automotive Quality Management System requirement known as ISO/TS 16949 (it's not really a full "Standard" but more correctly a "technical specification, under ISO's nomenclature), the various accreditation oversight bodies (AIAG, SMMT et al) have promoted the use of what is known as the "turtle diagram."

This audit tool was heavily based upon an original idea by the US quality guru, Phil Crosby, which he proposed as his "Process Control Worksheet"[4].

The Crosby Process Worksheet takes the "SIPOC" model (Supplier, Input, Process, Output, Customer) and adds "requirements" to the input and output. Further, to the Process are applied training, measurement (of product and process), equipment, and procedures. These may be thought of as the four basic "arms" of the Ishikawa or "fishbone" diagram for cause analysis of a problem, the so-called "4Ms," which are Materials, Machines, Man, and Methods.

Turtle diagrams were introduced as a means to encourage Certification Body auditors to plan audits of clients' quality management systems in terms of processes – what has become known as the "automotive process approach" to audits. During so-called "witness audits" by the automotive accreditation oversight body, it was noted that (some) certification body auditors were performing their audits by addressing discrete elements or clauses of the requirements document (in this case the predecessor of ISO/TS 16949, QS-9000). This was thought to be ineffective, since no "linkages" were evaluated, for example, between the product design process and manufacturing – an interface that, among others, often has weaknesses. Recently, the aerospace industry oversight bodies have also adopted the turtle diagram as an audit planning tool, despite no evidence that auditors were not employing a process approach to their audits.

---

[4]Permission to replicate the worksheet was not provided.

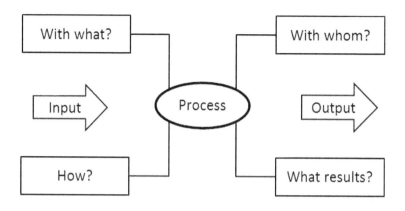

As a planning tool, the turtle diagram has some benefits to those who may have only experienced clause- or element-type audits. However, there is a significant issue with the use of this planning tool – the *effect of the "sequence and interaction" of other processes on the subject process being audited is not addressed.* It is this interaction between processes that has been shown to be a key component of effective management systems. Since understanding the key relationship(s) between processes is vital to understanding controls and their effectiveness, having a plan to evaluate them at the appropriate time during the audit is important.

Clearly, if an audit is to be conducted with more than simple compliance to an international Standard as the objective, a different type of "checklist" – or other type of planning tool – should be employed, to assist the auditor in understanding the audit task, and in preparing for a complete audit.

We know that a process can be defined as "activities that transform inputs into outputs." One might add, "under controlled conditions," since we usually want to be able to predict a (good) result! From this definition, we already know any process has:

- input(s)
- output(s)
- activities
- controls

This is helpful, but heading off to do an internal audit armed with a checklist with just four topics is unlikely to help us reveal if the process is working as intended. As auditors, we have to develop a better understanding of what an effective process requires to deliver a satisfactory outcome for the organization and its customers.

Most business processes have some form of goal or objective assigned to them, so that performance can be determined. This might be focused externally on customers' needs or internally to the organization. And it's usual that these goals and objectives have a measurement associated with them. If the process is working effectively, it's by these performance criteria that an auditor can tell what's being achieved.

In addition, it's desirable to produce a consistent result; therefore, the process must be under control. Most of us know the wailing sound (output) made by a loudspeaker, when the microphone (input) is placed too close to that speaker – it's called feedback! You can certainly measure the sound level, but the process is out of control! Our business processes need controls to ensure things don't get out of hand. Process controls for the activities are accomplished in many ways:

- people – competent, aware and trained
- equipment – (preventive) maintenance (calibrated, if necessary for measurement)

- methods – procedures, work instructions (as necessary, under document control)
- materials – approved, available, identified, and so on

In considering these control criteria, our list of audit topics has grown quickly, and we must also consider some other controls that must be in place – documentation controls, non-conformance, records generated from the process, corrective/preventive actions, and improvements.

The "Football©" Planning Tool

The challenge of preparing for any audit is the sequence in which to place these, so that we can gather useful information about the process, rather than just a number of facts, since creating a simple list of these topics is not as helpful. A number of "visual metaphors" have been used as tools to assist auditors. One unique approach has proven successful in helping auditors to organize these topics in an appropriate sequence – the "Football©." (See appendix Y.)

The use of this tool to "visualize" the path an internal auditor should take when auditing a process has a number of advantages:

- Comprehensive planning – so that all relevant controls are considered, in their correct sequence (the preceding is an example applicable to a manufacturing process).
- Structure to audit checklists or questions – they follow the appropriate process flow. This allows information to be gathered and used later to verify performance.
- It can assist an audit manager with ensuring the assigned auditor (s) do the relevant research of those requirements and controls, so that they develop better understanding of them, before the audit interviews.

- The auditor has a "bigger picture" to audit and is therefore more likely to see systematic issues.

- Evaluation of actual process performance against the objective(s) as well as compliance to the QMS.

- Better time management, adherence to audit scope and so on. By populating the various "bubbles" (in the example) with the details of the organization's management system and/or customer requirements and so on, the auditor is able to get a clearer understanding of the expected outcomes. They are better able to identify opportunities within the management systems, as a result.

It is often easy for an internal auditor to be "drawn off track" when evaluating the other criteria and controls (depicted by the football's "laces"), which can affect a process – personnel training, for example – and the football assists the auditor in defining the "boundaries," at which point they must decide to return to the normal process flow.

If, in preparing for their audit, the auditor solicits input to the planning activities of the affected management and frame their focus of the audit to include risk (the "effect of uncertainty on objectives"), they may well learn of issues not previously considered by other planning techniques. Often, individuals can be found who have a significant stake in the performance of a process and anything that may have an adverse effect on the achievement of the goals and objectives set for that process.

For example, having deliveries from a new supplier, held in Receiving Inspection due to a detected problem, may stimulate the interest of the Material Controls/Production Planning function – if the Production Department's goals of delivering a specific quantity of products to meet sales demand is at risk.

In review then, conducting process-based internal Quality Management System audits can be an overwhelming task, leading to a report that is based only on a consideration of compliance. The use of a planning tool like the football, to map out an auditor's strategy, leads to far more effective and efficient audits and focuses the auditor on validating the results of the process, to management's plan.

Instead of just being a set of questions to ask (often in the form of the checklist, previously described), an auditor should have a clear guide to the "answers" to their questioning, which come from studying and comprehending the audit assignment they are given.

Audit execution

Opening Meetings

Conventions, particularly for external audits, require that an opening meeting be held with the auditee at the start of the audit. The following topics are usually included in the agenda:

- Introductions of the auditor(s) and the organization's participants.
- Purpose of meeting and audit scope.
- Review of audit agenda/changes.
- Logistics: workspace, meal arrangements, working hours, and so on.
- Use of, and availability of, safety equipment.
- Audit guides.
- Audit process: interviews, evidence gathering, and so on.
- Audit reporting: verbal, written, grading.

- Daily reviews (if multi-day audit).
- Confidentiality statement.
- Closing meeting purpose and timing.
- Discussion/Q&A.

This agenda may seem somewhat "heavy" or overly formal for the purposes of an internal management systems audit, and an abbreviated version may include just some basic features, described in the next section.

Introductions

It is essential and good workplace protocol when an auditor enters any workspace or location to introduce themselves to the relevant management or supervision, because:

- The person conducting the audit is usually recognized as being in their usual job and management may not be aware of their purpose in performing the audit – in short, it may look as if the person is "goofing off."
- Since the auditor is likely to be known by the auditee, it serves to ensure they will now "see" the person as an auditor, with different behaviors, different work purpose.
- It's important to engage management and their support for the audit, including any actions that may arise from it.
- It sets the "tone" for the audit and is seen to involve management and therefore be seen as important by the people who work in the area.

By reference to the preceding agenda topics, a more appropriate internal audit opening meeting may cover:

- Introductions of the auditor(s) and the organization's participants.

- Purpose of audit as a tool to identify risk(s).
- Review of audit scope, audit agenda/changes.
- Closing meeting purpose and timing.
- Discussion of actionable items.

Audit interviews

At some point, shortly after the "opening meeting" is conducted, it is normal to begin the process of interviewing people responsible for, and involved in, the subject process.

Armed with a checklist (if chosen for use), it may be tempting for the auditor to begin by reading questions directly from the sheet. If these questions are based on a rephrasing of the Standard, for example, "Has the organization established, implemented, maintained, and improved the processes of the Quality Management System?" Phrasing questions in a closed manner, like this, is a key teaching point in various auditor training courses – closed questions are often referred to as "Kipling's Serving Men" and include "who, how, what, when, and where." Since these types of questions are specifically intended to get the interviewee to give more than a "yes" or "no" response, the result of phrasing a global question, such as the preceding one, is in most cases impossible.

Such an approach is unlikely to reveal very much to anyone, least of all from the person being audited. Indeed, this type of question might, in fact, be better answered at the conclusion of the audit, rather than at the very outset.

Without a robust reply from the person being interviewed, the auditor may feel they didn't ask the "right thing," leading to confusion and panic. The auditee may feel confused, and even annoyed, at not being able to respond appropriately.

If the auditor has planned and prepared their own set of topics to interview someone about, there's likely to be less frustration in phrasing a question. Having researched the subject process and the related objectives and measurement(s) applied to the process, the auditor's own notes about those topics then become the basis of their inquiry, and, as a result, their questioning becomes a much simpler task:

> *"Tell me about/describe to me the process," then, "What are the objectives?" Followed by, "What results are you currently getting?"*

If these questions are directed, initially at the process owner (or similar), it is highly likely that they are experienced in being asked – and hence answering – the same thing by their management! In which case, a complete answer is likely to be forthcoming, since the question uses terminology which is that of the person interviewed.

Compare the preceding question with one based on an ISO requirement:

> *"Has the organization established quality objectives at relevant levels?"*

Evidence gathering

Since the audit has a clearly stated scope and criterion, the evidence gathered by an internal auditor should be focused on these, specifically to determine where the risks (if any) might lay. That is not to say the auditor should become oblivious or ignore anything not within their remit, of course. This focus also deals with another perennial problem of "sampling" that plagues audit techniques based on external methods. Questions arising include:

How many items should be sampled?
Should a statistically based sampling plan be used?
If a non-conformity is found, should further samples be taken?

By narrowing the focus of the audits, the sample becomes self-evident and these imponderable questions become immaterial.

Audit Reporting

Since a lot of effort has been put into planning, preparing, and conducting the audit, it is similarly important to report the results of the audit in a manner that management will be able to understand. From what is reported it will be necessary to identify any actions necessary to remediate the observed situation(s). Since the fundamentals of management systems auditing is based on the external audit model, it follows that the reporting is also based on this model.

Audit Non-conformity Reports

If we refer back to the descriptions of supplier audits earlier in the book, we can see that supplier quality was controlled through the adherence to a set of requirements, often either a controlling document such as a Supplier Quality Handbook or a contract/product-specific quality plan called a control plan, service level agreement, or similar. During such supplier audits, observations made where there was deviation from these requirements, the auditors issued what are generally known as "Non-conformity Reports" (NCRs) or "Corrective Actions Requests" (CARs). Characteristically, NCRs or CARs detail the specifics of the auditor's observations, made from watching people perform their tasks, from their studying of documentation/records, and interviews with the supplier's personnel. Often the content of the non-conformity reports is compliance oriented:

> *"On the assembly line, it was observed that the operators were not following the assembly instructions."*

Or:

> *"The internal auditors didn't follow the audit procedure SOP822 rev a, because the checklist wasn't in evidence."*

Although simple compliance statements may be accurate, they are often unhelpful to those who are responsible for taking action in response to them!

Reporting that someone "didn't follow procedure" is just a symptom, pure and simple. To get management's attention and support for action to address what is being reported, it is the auditor's responsibility to frame the issue in terms that communicate the risk(s) associated with what was observed. In order to do this, further examination is necessary by the auditor, to identify what the results of not following the documentation cause or create – if any.

Grading of Audit Non-conformities

Another part of the tradition of reporting audits, which comes from the world of supplier assessments, is the practice of grading the non-conformity reports. Although ISO19011 (and even ISO/IEC 17021 for Certification Bodies) mentions this aspect of audit reporting in notes only, it is a common practice across all types of audits to give an audit report of non-conformity some form of label indicating severity. This grading often follows these conventions:

> Critical, Major, or Minor
> Hold Point
> "Met," "Not met," "Partially met"
> Grade "A," "B," "C," and so on
> Category "1," "2," and so on
> Stop Work Order

The more commonly employed grades of "major" and "minor" usually carry definitions similar to these[5]:

Major:

> *The absence or total breakdown of a system to meet the ISO9000 requirement.*
> *A number of minor nonconformities against one requirement can represent a total breakdown of the system and thus be considered a major nonconformity.*
> *Any noncompliance that would result in the probable shipment of nonconforming product.*
> *A condition that may result in the failure or materially reduce the usability of the products or services for their intended purpose.*
> *A noncompliance that judgment and experience indicate is likely either to result in the failure of the*

---

quality system or to materially reduce its ability to assure controlled processes or products.

Minor:

An ISO9000 nonconformance to that judgment and experience indicate is not likely to result in the failure of the quality system or reduce its ability to assure controlled processes or products.
A failure in some part of the supplier's documented quality system relative to ISO9000, or
A single observed lapse in following one item of the company's quality system.

As we can see, grading of audit non-conformities has its roots in the world of supplier evaluation and addresses the need to define the significance of the non-conformance(s). In grading the non-conformity(ies) the readers of the audit report may better understand the conclusion drawn by the auditor(s).

For example, a (manufacturing) supplier who is evaluated to have major non-conformities relating to the control of its measuring equipment might be considered as a source only after they take corrective action or while under supplier development support to remediate the situation. The action may include providing the supplier with calibrated gauges to be used on the purchased product.

The auditor will complete a non-conformity report (form) with the following fundamental information:

- the source of the audit requirement
- the audit requirement
- the source of the audit evidence and
- the audit evidence observed.

An example non-conformity report statement might read as follows:

> "The organization's calibration procedure CAL-001, revision #2, states in paragraph 8.3.1, that reviews are performed and recorded on received calibration reports, to identify any out of tolerance conditions that may exist. The record is annotated in the equipment record. (Gagetrak)
>
> The reports for micrometers MIC028 and MIC036 show that for the last calibration, the flatness of the anvil (028) and zero point (036) were out of specification as received by the cal. lab. No evidence of review or subsequent actions of these conditions has been recorded."

In addition to the reporting of non-conformities, it is also common practice to report issues observed by auditors that are thought to indicate the potential for non-conformity. These are often known as an "observation," or "opportunity for improvement" (OFI). The use of observations and opportunities for improvement are thought to have come from Certification Bodies in their attempt to bring an "added value" to their services (or to make the issue more palatable to the client), which are traditionally simple compliance audits. Indeed, the third-party certification scheme associated with the automotive supplier requirements, known as "QS-9000," encouraged certification body auditors to report situations that fit the following definition:

> *"A noncompliance that judgment and experience indicate is likely either to result in the failure of the quality system or to materially reduce its ability to assure controlled processes or products."*

Although a well-constructed non-conformity report should convey to the organization the issue in need of action, it may be a stretch for those reading it to determine the risks associated with the reported condition. Furthermore, the principles of auditing based on an external model (supply chain or Conformity Assessment) tend to dictate that when an issue is discovered, the auditor will likely adopt the "iceberg principle," which posits that if the auditor can spend a relatively short amount of time to discover the issue, there's likely to be more that will need working on (below the "surface").

This approach has created the situation where corrective action is required for each and every audit finding. Indeed, many audit programs use a "Corrective Action Request" form to report the issue to management. In the preceding example, the need for action to investigate the effect on the measurements is passed on to the organization, instead of the auditor doing some more evaluation. For an external auditor, this "Iceberg" approach is simply because there isn't sufficient time to evaluate the situation! The micrometer being out of specification becomes a simple "non-conformity to requirements" statement and is considered through the eyes of the external auditor as "If I found it, then there's likely to be more like this."

We should not overlook that, when this aspect of reporting external audits was developed, the use of formal, third-party certified (quality) management systems weren't yet implemented. As a result, the context of reporting had to identify issues as being significant to the assurance of (product) quality, hence, requiring action to meet the customers' needs.

Since internal auditors have the potential to research, in greater detail, the background to the audit assignment, including discussions with management, review of performance metrics and so on, there should be a greater opportunity to "dig" into the management system issues both before the audit is conducted – in the planning and preparation for the audit – and then, as the need for investigation is identified, during the audits.

Where's the risk?

There is an opportunity to transform the reporting of audit results in a manner that conveys risks encountered in a direct and clear manner to management, to ensure they understand and, hence, take action appropriately. Too often, particularly when reporting "procedure not followed," there is little/no indication of what course of action should be taken: correction or corrective action.

Since the planning of the audit has been based on "status and importance" – now renamed as "risk and impact" – experience has shown the writing of a report that also makes reference to risk and impact is helpful to management.

Take the following example:

During an internal audit, it was discovered that products were awaiting shipment, which had been delayed, beyond the date agreed with the customer, because a key piece of information was missing. This information was supplied by the HQ organization, many miles from the production site.

This vital detail could only be mailed, as it included a sticker that had, by law, to be affixed to the packaging.

The auditors were instructed to report the finding in terms of risk and the impact (on the customer), as follows:

> *"A shipment of X cartons of NNNN product is held in the shipping department, because the required "V" stickers have not arrived from HQ. Failure to ship on time with a sticker will present a risk of customer dissatisfaction, and also increase shipping costs, since the stickers and product have to be expedited."*

In another scenario, it was found that product weights were found to be inaccurate, since the "check weigher" machine – used to test packaged product at the end of the production line – had not been verified to the required minimum weight (required by law). Again, the internal auditors were challenged to present the results to management in terms of risk:

> *"The check weighing machine on production line 'A' has not been verified as accurate in weighing product to the minimum value, required by law. Failure to assure a minimum weight presents the risks of regulatory compliance, customer complaints, and providing more product than the minimum required."*

Audit Summary Reports

At the conclusion of the audit, it is usual to provide management with a summary of the audit. The summary usually provides a platform for an encompassing description, often putting into context the individual incidents reported as non-conformities as well as the auditors' observations and conclusions from performing the audit.

The audit report may conclude for management the degree of compliance of the management system implementation and, hence, with an ISO Standard. A typical report may include the following example texts:

"During the internal audit, a total of five 'minor' non-conformities were discovered, affecting ISO9001 clauses 4.5.2, 4.5.3, 6.2.2, 7.6, and 8.3. Everyone interviewed seemed to understand their jobs and could state the quality policy. There were two OFIs where one box of product had a torn ID tag and a calibration sticker was missing from a gauge."

One has to ask, would anyone really lose sleep on reading this?

Where's the risk?

Summary reports are a convenient place for the auditor to make recommendations for the audit program to shift emphasis, based upon the findings. Indeed, the 2000 version of ISO9004 stated as much!

"Planning for internal audits should be flexible in order to permit changes in emphasis based on findings and objective evidence obtained during the audit"

This practical guidance is, sadly, missing from the current revision of the guidance and experience shows, furthermore, that it is rarely incorporated into any internal management systems audit procedure.

If a process approach to audits are adopted (see the "Football© diagram), it can be seen that many supporting processes can be evaluated during a specific audit. If there are observations of concerns/risks relating to one or more of these supporting processes, it may be suggested that a future audit be used to further evaluate the situation. This is particularly important since there is rarely opportunity to follow an audit trail, in pursuit of an item of interest to the audit. If the natural "trail" is followed, it would take the auditor "out of scope" and may lead to further problems with the actual conduct of the audit program as a whole.

Examples may include such supporting processes as document and records controls, control of non-conforming product, control of measurement equipment, and so on. Following up on a trail relating to these processes will, inevitably, take the hapless auditor off to another physical location and so on (the metrology lab, document controller, IT department etc.), where the employees weren't prepared to be audited!

These approaches to reporting audit findings are predominantly based on external audit techniques that are somewhat out of alignment with the needs of the organization's management needs. Furthermore, they are unlikely to promote an effective internal management systems audit program, which makes the transition along the maturity curve shown in *Figure 1*.

Since a great deal of the protocols of what is taught in auditor courses and, indeed, much of the content of ISO19011, is formulated upon external audit techniques, they can seem somewhat like "fitting a square peg into a round hole."

When an organization is seeking third-party certification, it is not unusual for the CB auditor to recognize internal management audit programs that closely follow what has been described previously – since it is highly likely the auditor undertook the same type of training (the Lead Auditor course). Such audit programs are characterized by:

- An annual calendar of audits.
- Auditors selected without reference to business process knowledge or competency.
- Minimal planning and preparation by the assigned auditor(s).
- Lack of involvement by management in audit process.
- Compliance-oriented audit non-conformity reports, which state clauses of the ISO Standard.
- Lack of management support for audit findings needing action.
- Few recommendations of changes to audit plan based on what's observed as "risks."

One might conclude, therefore, that internal audits initially possess more "style than substance."

It is important for internal audit programs to mature beyond simple compliance and meeting external auditor expectations, to a situation where the focus of audits becomes those issues that are relevant to management's interests:

- customers' requirements
- regulatory compliance
- (cost) effectiveness and efficiency

After the Audit

As with many aspects of external audits, there is an expectation of some form of action as a result of the internal audit. After all, if there was something to report to management, it should be important enough to do something about it!

In the context of an external audit, (supply chain or Conformity Assessment), when an issue is discovered, the auditor will likely adopt the "iceberg principle," which posits that if the auditor can spend a relatively short amount of time to discover the issue, there's likely to be more that will need working on (below the "surface").

This approach has created the situation where corrective action is required for each and every audit finding. Indeed, many audit programs use a "Corrective Action Request" form to report the issue to management.

Correction versus Corrective Action

A further "legacy" of the use of a Corrective Action Request is that an expectation is established for some form of structured "root cause" analysis to be performed in response to the reported non-conformities. Root cause analysis may include such methodologies as "8D," "5

Whys," Kepner-Tragoe" Analysis, or similar. This often leads to the proverbial "sledgehammer to crack a nut," when the real course of action may be a simple correction of the reported issue. See *pages 86–87*.

The system for tracking and reporting the status of the corrective actions process may, subsequently, be inundated by an impossible number of corrective actions. Instead of using Pareto Analysis (the 80/20 Rule) to separate out those systematic issues that may need, indeed, require a root cause corrective action, everything is given the same priority and eventually the process grinds to a halt – with the result that internal auditors are frequently critical of management failing to take their audit reports "seriously."

By addressing risk in the audit reporting methods (instead of quoting requirements from ISO standards, or stating a "procedure wasn't followed"), auditors automatically create opportunities where the correction versus corrective action requirement become obvious.

CHAPTER 4: THIRD-PARTY CERTIFICATION OF MANAGEMENT SYSTEMS

Although the primary focus of this book is that of internal management systems audits, many organizations that implement the requirements of one or more of the international ISO standards often also choose to be certified by a so-called "third party." To enable some comparison and, therefore, to be able to contrast audit styles, this chapter is included and describes the background to the development of "third-party certification of management systems," or what's more commonly known as "ISO certification." This term is, in fact, somewhat misleading since the ISO organization doesn't involve itself in any aspect of the certification process.

Although not required to be successful in implementing an ISO-based management system, an independent certification of compliance is a common option for many organizations. Often, major purchasing organizations in the aerospace, automotive, defense, and medical device industries require their direct suppliers to obtain an independent certification to ISO9001 as a minimum before contracts are awarded. This requirement is often handed down the line to lower-tier suppliers.

Unless specifically required to comply with customer or regulatory requirements, an organization may either choose a self-declaration of compliance with an ISO management system Standard or choose to have a significant customer attest to the same. These aren't usually as acceptable to discerning customers, or for other reasons, as the option of an independent certification audit performed by an accredited certification body/registrar.

Before we scrutinize the role and processes of a certification body, it is worth spending some time understanding aspects of accreditation or oversight that govern their operation in the marketplace.

The Importance of Accreditation of Certification Bodies

Accreditation of certification bodies is seemingly not well understood by those who have to employ certification services, despite it being of vital importance to the credibility and quality of the resulting audits. Some basic information about the influence accreditation has on the certification body and its processes is very important to any organization considering offering its QMS for certification. If accreditation of an organization's ISO9000 certification is not recognized by a customer, it may mean starting back at square one, with the costs being doubled.

Accreditation of certification bodies started in the UK in the late 1980s, shortly after ISO9001 was made publicly available. In response to a (1977) UK Government white paper, written by Sir Frederick Warner, entitled "Standards and Specifications in the Engineering Industries," which identified the opportunity to reduce the costs and disruption associated with multiple supplier audits of the same suppliers, the concept of using an independent body to certify compliance with the (appropriate) international Standard was floated.

To ensure a minimum level of consistency between what became known as "certification bodies," the UK Government established an oversight or accreditation body titled the National Accreditation Council for Certification Bodies (NACCB). A similar accreditation body was also established in the Netherlands, known as the Raad Voor Certificatie (RVC). These organizations are currently known as UKAS (United Kingdom Accreditation Service) and RVA (Raad Voor Accreditatie), having changed their names to better describe their activities. Other nations followed suit as ISO9000 gained acceptance around the globe, including the US, where today the principle American national accreditation body – the American National Accreditation Body (ANAB) – is run jointly by the American National Standards Institute (ANSI) and the American Society for Quality (ASQ).

Accreditation bodies evaluate and monitor the performance of certification bodies (as well as other, similar organizations) against a set of defined requirements, from another ISO Standard, this time ISO/IEC 17021. They ensure the audits are carried out according to defined processes and criteria, including the competence of auditors. Applying ISO/IEC 17021 to a certification body is not unlike an organization implementing ISO9000 for its products. Both standards are employed to ensure a quality output from the organization's business processes.

Today, accreditation of certification bodies is managed, typically, on a national basis, by each organization's country. Some exceptions exist in the automobile industry, where the IATF (International Automotive Task Force) oversees Third-party Certification Bodies providing ISO/TS 16949 certification and APMG provides accreditation for the Information Services Standard ISO/IEC 20000 as an alternative to ANAB. For the purposes of this book, the descriptions will focus on the accreditation of management systems by ANAB.

To ensure consistency across nations, accreditation bodies may subscribe to the International Accreditation Forum (IAF), which, through multilateral agreements, provides oversight of the certification bodies. In addition to the requirement of ISO/IEC 17021, the IAF also publishes a number of documents, including tables that define the number of days an audit should take, based on the number of people (headcount) involved in the organization's QMS. For example, the IAF's MD5 table can be found on the IAF.nu website and also includes descriptions of the factors that allow for tailoring of audit time. Organizations considering certification can obtain this "insider information" to ensure their quoted audit duration is appropriate.

Certification body services

When selecting a certification body (CB), the default supplier selection process often starts with getting three quotes. Quotes may be solicited from these three certification bodies, and, once they're received, a review might reveal ... nothing, except the amounts of time for the audit (in days, usually), and therefore costs, appear to be very similar. For ISO9001 and ISO14001 certification audits, the IAF's MD5 document defines the duration of each audit, primarily based upon the headcount of the organization. For certification schemes, such as the IATF's ISO/TS 16949, the audit duration is defined in a supporting document, issued by the IATF, "The rules for achieving ISO/TS Certification." For the aerospace sector, the International Aerospace Quality Group (IAQG) publishes the AS9101 document covering multiple rules for certification, including audit duration.

The other (typical) costs associated with the auditing service will relate to the following (typical) factors:

- auditor daily rate
- fees, labeled "admin" or "account management" and
- fees for reviewing corrective actions arising from any non-conformity reports issuing from an audit'
- travel time (sometimes billed)

Possibly the most significant of these costs is the auditor daily rate, since this may be a key indicator of the amount the auditor charges the CB (many auditors are subcontractors, not employees), or perhaps how much the CB is prepared to pay the auditor. Many auditors are listed by the body they are certified through, for example, RABQSA, in an online directory. It may be that the chosen CB selects a candidate auditor only from that list, without consideration of any other characteristics than the qualifications needed to be on the list!

Another question to be asked might also be whether the auditor is local to the client's premises. Although an auditor being "around the corner" is optimal in keeping travel expenses lower, this doesn't consider the following two facets:

- The auditor who is local may not possess the necessary experience (EAC code) to suit the client's business type.
- There may be an auditor who is scheduled in the area to perform other audits and, therefore, travel expenses can be amortized across a number of clients. If a client is flexible about audit dates, such an arrangement can work well.

It's not unusual for an organization to send a list of questions to be answered by certification bodies, as input to the selection process. The following are some typical points that have been asked of certification body candidates:

- Who are you accredited with, and are they accredited by a signatory to the IAF, or ANAB-accredited?
- Do you publish an official interpretation of the ISO requirements and can we get a copy?
- Have you ever had your accreditation revoked or suspended? If so, what were the circumstances?
- Share the number of local clients in our area.
- Detail your experience in auditing facilities such as machining job shops.
- Share the number of local lead auditors in our area.
- Detail the experiences of these lead auditors in auditing facilities such as machining job shops.
- Detail the number of lead auditors available for the auditing and maintenance of our certification.
- How flexible are you on scheduling or rescheduling?
- How do you handle differences of opinion over interpretation of the Standard?
- What is the process of handling differences, and whom do we contact?
- Is the stage 1 audit conducted on-site, off-site, or a combination?
- How fast can we set up an interview with you?
- Can we also set up an interview with the lead auditor who would be assigned to us?

If we take a look at these questions, many could have been answered at the same time as question one was answered –

and that could be simply answered by a quick check of the IAF website! Accreditation to ISO/IEC 17021 takes care of issues such as auditor qualifications, appeals, conduct of the stage 1 audit, and so on.

Perhaps it's interesting to note that such questionnaires completely miss many of the points that really affect the actual relationship an organization will likely have with its chosen certification body! Rather than waste time asking questions that are actually answered by their accreditation – which is a "playing field leveler" – it would be better to address the actual performance of the certification body in delivering more than just an audit and certificate of compliance with an ISO Standard!

Let's consider what aspects of the services provided by a CB impact the organization:

- quality of service (technical, scheduling, value of audit reports)
- quality of auditors (competence, industry experience, audit approach, professionalism)
- credibility or reputation of certification (how do your customers and other certified clients perceive the CB?)

Having selected a certification body, the process begins with providing information about the organization on which a quotation may be based.

Typically, the information required by the CB, on which it bases its quote, includes:

- Contact personnel details.
- Names, positions, phone numbers, e-mail addresses, fax numbers.

- Organization details:
  - o Name, street address (HQ).
  - o Other locations (if applicable).
- Headcount involved in the management system.
- The scope of the management system.
- Exclusions from the management system (where permitted), such as design, customer property, control of measuring equipment.

The quotation or proposal is likely to reflect the amount of audit time for the following activities:

- the "stage 1" audit
- the "stage 2" audit
- the surveillance audit (usually annually) and
- the "triennial reassessment"

It is common for a third-party certificate to be valid for three years. This is a legacy of the approvals given by the UK's Ministry of Defence (MoD) to its suppliers. Early adopters of third-party certification, in the early 1990s, were often suppliers to the UK MoD, the British Government, and various government departments, making it a requirement for them to be third-party certified.

Note – if a CB doesn't quote a cost and duration for the triennial audit, the guidance from ISO/IEC 17021 states that the audit is approximately two-thirds of the combined stage 1 two-audit durations.

The certification body will also issue some form of contractually binding agreement. This describes the terms and conditions relating to payment for its services, and details of the organization's commitment to the rules relating to certification of its Quality Management System. These rules are passed down, from the accreditation bodies, by the certification bodies, to their clients, and are defined (in part) in ISO/IEC 17021. Typically, the rules include:

- confidentiality of the information obtained about the organization
- changes relating to the organization's
  - o ownership
  - o management and
  - o locations
- changes relating to the
  - o scope of the management system in terms of products, services locations, for example, and
  - o major changes to the management system, including those affecting management, regulations, documents and so on; withdrawal of certification.

An additional audit service offered by most certification bodies is known as the "preliminary assessment" or "pre-assessment." This is a purely optional audit that is not part of the formal certification audit process; is usually a shorter-duration audit; and, as its name suggests, is performed before the actual certification audit is performed. This audit is described later.

Certification body audit process – the basics

Before the various types of audit conducted by a certification body are described in detail, it's worth taking a look at the basic activities at the core of these audits. These activities are normally founded on the requirement of ISO19011, "Guidelines for Auditing Management Systems."

The key components of the audit process include the following:

Opening meetings

At the scheduled time, according to the audit schedule/agenda (or other arrangements made), the assigned lead auditor will chair a meeting with representatives of the organization. An agenda for the meeting might look something like this:

- Introductions of the auditor(s) and the organization's participants.
- Purpose of meeting and audit scope.
- Review of audit agenda/changes.
- Logistics: workspace, meal arrangements, working hours, and so on.
- Audit guides.
- The need for, and availability of, safety equipment.
- Audit process: interviews, evidence gathering, and so on.
- Audit reporting: verbal, written, grading.
- Daily reviews (if multi-day audit).
- Confidentiality statement.
- Closing meeting purpose and timing.
- Discussion/Q & A.

Audit activities

On completion of the opening meeting, the auditor(s) will begin their audit assignments. The audit purpose is to verify that the organization's management system is implemented and is effective in achieving the stated objectives. They must "test" various people's understanding of their jobs and process controls, and determine that the organization is effectively planning for the results it and its customers expect to achieve.

To accomplish this, auditors will interview the relevant personnel, from management to members of staff and associates who perform work, asking questions about the processes they work on, the objective(s) of those processes, and current performance of those processes. The auditors will likely also ask questions intended to verify understanding of various people's responsibilities and authority for control of processes, including taking action when unplanned situations arise, perhaps resulting in nonconforming products, and so on.

Auditors make copious notes as they verify the evidence they see and hear, including references to the specific documents and records they request to see. These records will, typically, include customer orders/contracts, purchase orders placed on suppliers, competence evaluations and training records, minutes from product design review technical meetings, internal auditors' notes, and so on. These are compared to the organization's documented Quality Management System and, with what was learned from interviews, a picture is formed by the certification body auditor(s) as to the degree of compliance and effectiveness.

Closing meetings

At the conclusion of a certification body audit, whether it's stage 2, surveillance, or triennial reassessment, the auditor will convene a "closing meeting." The purpose of the meeting is to summarize the findings of the audit for the organization, to discuss any follow-up actions that may be necessary, and to outline the purpose and timing of the next visit.

At the end of the audit, one important action for the auditor is to deliver a recommendation to the organization, appropriate to the type of audit that has just been performed. The recommendation is based upon the evidence gathered and conclusions arrived at by the auditor(s).

Example recommendations are defined in the following descriptions of each audit type.

Audit reporting

Certification body auditors are required to fully report the results of the audits they perform. There are two basic forms of report:

- Non-conformity reports
- audit summary reports

Non-conformity reports (NCRs)

Non-conformity (non-conformance) reports are possibly the most interesting to the organization being audited. As the audit unfolds, the auditor may observe a situation or situations where evidence indicates the Quality Management System is not being implemented, or is not as effective as intended or planned.

In these situations, having agreed the facts with the organization's representatives, the auditor will complete a non-conformity report (form) with the following fundamental information:

- the source of the audit requirement
- the audit requirement
- the source of the audit evidence and
- the audit evidence observed

An example non-conformity report statement might read as follows:

> The organization's Quality Manual, revision #3, states in paragraph 3.3.1, that management reviews are held with a minimum of three Vice Presidents (Engineering, Production, and Quality) in attendance at a meeting to discuss process performance to objectives.

> The minutes (record) of the review meeting held on 31 January 2012, indicates that only two VPs were in attendance (Engineering and Quality). As a result, there was no review of Production-related performance to objectives.

> The SLA for ACME states a helpdesk initial response to the client will be made within 15 min of receiving a help request. In the period July 5–July 8, it was noted that approximately 25% of responses were made after the 15-min limit.

The nature of the content of each non-conformity report is reviewed and graded by the auditor. Grading gives "gravity" to the content of the report as a means to communicate significance. It is typical that a certification body auditor will consider whether what's been observed is an isolated or localized non-conformity, not indicating a systemic issue, or whether the situation is determined to be a breakdown of the Quality Management System. Such a breakdown might be a failure of effectiveness, a failure to implement, or a significant number of the (initially) localized non-conformities clustered around a specific ISO9001 requirement.

In an ISO9001 certification audit, there are no specific "rules" for determining when a number of observed non-conformities warrant classification as either "minor" or "major." A certification body may have its own definitions of categories of non-conformity reports, including "major," "minor," "opportunity for improvement," "category 1," "category 2" and so on, and some even have definitions of how many "minor" non-conformities found constitute a "major" non-conformity, in their certification service agreement or contract.

A common feature of Certification Body audit non-conformity reports is the inclusion of a statement of the effectiveness of the process/system being audited.

The requirements for auditors to report on this (important) aspect comes from both the automotive and aerospace oversight schemes for Certification Bodies (the "IATF" and "IAQG").

Audit summary reports

The certification body auditor is required to demonstrate that a comprehensive audit has been carried out, so, toward the end of the audit, a summary of the audit is completed. The certification body will provide the auditor with a form in a prepared format that is then filled out with the details of the specific audit. Details are completed based on the notes taken, people (job titles) interviewed, records reviewed, and so forth.

The summary report will also contain a recommendation to the certification body's management on the status of the organization's management system and whether a certificate of compliance should be issued.

The preliminary or pre-assessment audit

Since most organizations come to ISO certification without significant experience of the audit process, the preliminary assessment can be a very useful experience. For readers who are familiar with the performing arts, it's quite normal, immediately before the "first night" of the performance, for the performers to have a "dry run" through their performance, in the venue, with other performers, musicians, and so on. This dry run is often referred to as the "dress rehearsal" and is done to make any final adjustments to the performance before the public get to see and critique it.

A dress rehcarsal isn't to make major adjustments to the score, choreography, costumes, and so on, since there's no time available. Instead, it gives the producers an opportunity to visualize the performance in situ, and, hence, minor adjustments may be identified and accommodated.

Unlike the "stage 1" and "stage 2" audits, there is no defined duration for the preliminary assessment, so the organization can choose how long it believes is needed. What's more, the organization gets to decide what it wants the auditor to review during the visit. The agenda is theirs to define. An organization may decide to have the auditor focus on a few aspects, or take a sweep of the entire Quality Management System. In selecting a smaller focus, organizations often are interested in those aspects of the QMS that may be new to them, for example, a calibration system, where none was formally defined or implemented before. Often, a broad view of the status of the system as a whole can validate for the management team that their efforts are, indeed, ready to undergo the more detailed scrutiny of the registration audit. It acts, therefore, as a dress rehearsal for the actual certification audit.

Other benefits include:

- Observing how the assigned certification body auditor goes about performing the audit.

Although the organization will have conducted internal audits, it's always good to know how the CB auditor does things.

- Observing how they interact with the various people they interview.

Each CB auditor is different and they have unique ways of establishing good communications with the people they interact with. It helps to "break the ice" if you know this ahead of time.

- Allowing various (key) people of the organization to experience being audited by the certification body auditor.

As before, although internal audits will have been performed, not everyone will have had a role in those. Some people might be natural candidates to be audited by the CB auditor, and it's a great time to give them that experience.

- Uncovering a potential weakness in the system before the stage 2 audit.

This is very useful, of course, as the auditor who did the preliminary assessment will be very aware of the actions you took to rectify the situation found, which also builds confidence in the commitment to implementing an effective system.

The preliminary assessment can be timed with the stage 1 audit. This allows for some continuity of understanding for the auditor since they will have been able to study your system documentation and, while that knowledge is still "fresh," to take a look at aspects of the implementation too. It also helps to cut down on expenses!

The results of the preliminary assessment can be a useful input to the "management review" as a formal indicator of the "suitability and effectiveness" of the Quality Management System, in the days leading up to the registration audit. Any report from the preliminary assessment is not supposed to have any impact on the actual certification audit, it being entirely up to the organization's management to determine if any of the auditor's reported comments are significant enough to warrant corrective actions. In actual fact, if the same auditor who did the preliminary assessment performs the stage 2, then, if the client chooses to act on the auditor's comments and observations, it will be noticed and will possibly be viewed positively by the auditor, as validation.

A recommendation from the preliminary assessment is whether the client's QMS is in a suitable status to be successful at the certification audit.

The stage 1 audit

On a mutually agreed date, the certification body's assigned auditor (also known as the "lead auditor") performs what is known as the stage 1 audit. The purpose of carrying out this audit is defined in ISO/IEC 17021 as being:

- To evaluate the documented Quality Management System.

- To ensure the Standard's requirements have been understood and that key performance, processes, objectives, and operation have all been identified.

- To verify the information collected regarding the Quality Management System's scope and processes, the locations of the business, and any related regulatory and statutory compliance issues.

- To review and agree the duration and timing of the stage 2 audit.

- To plan the audit activities of the stage 2 audit.

- To ensure the internal audits and management reviews have been carried out and that there's sufficient implementation to support readiness to undergo the stage 2 audit.

The stage 1 audit includes a report detailing the preceding, plus any findings from the audit of documentation and so on.

As well as this report, another key output of the stage 1 audit is a plan or agenda for the stage 2 audit. That plan will, typically, detail each individual focus of the Quality Management System with the duration, timing, and auditor assignments. It may look something like this example (for an organization designing and manufacturing pumps) for a team of two auditors:

Monday, April 4	**Lead auditor – audit activity**	**Auditor 2 – audit activity**
8.00 am	Opening meeting with management	

8.30 am	Overview of QMS, objectives, and key measurements	
9.00 am	Proposals and contracts processing*	Product design and development*
10.00 am	Production planning	
11.00 am	Purchasing process, incl. outsourcing controls*	
12.00 pm	Lunch	
12.30 pm	Receiving and inspection*	Quality planning and controls*
1.00 pm	Manufacturing process – housing machining*	Manufacturing process – casting*
2.00 pm	Pump assembly*	Manufacturing process – impeller machining*
2.45 pm	Pump testing*	Inventory control and warehousing*
3.15 pm	Non-conforming product controls*	Pump finishing*
4.00 pm	Review and compilation of day's findings	
4.30 pm	Presentation of day's findings and day 2 schedule/adjustments	
5.00 pm	Auditors depart	

Tuesday, April 5	Lead auditor – audit activity	Auditor 2 – audit activity
8.00 am	Calibration of measuring equipment*	Pump packaging/ shipping
8.45 am	Customer feedback and satisfaction*	Equipment maintenance*
9.15 am	Internal audits*	Personnel training programs
10.00 am	Corrective action*	Product and process improvement*
11.00 am	Continuous improvement activities	
12.00 pm	Lunch and discussions	
12.45 pm	Management review	
1.00 pm	Audit findings analysis and report preparation	
2.00 pm	Closing meeting	
3.00 pm	Auditors depart	

Audit activities will also consider relevant controls of documentation, records, product status, measurements, monitoring, personnel competences, and data analysis.

Once the stage 1 audit is completed, the organization should be clear about the next steps and timing of the stage 2 audit, plus any actions necessary to address issues arising from the audit. Typically, this means taking corrective actions on items raised by the auditor that can affect the successful outcome of the stage 2 audit. A formal submission of actions to the certification body is not usually required, since they will be verified as part of stage 2.

The recommendation from this audit relates to the state of preparation of the client's QMS to undergo the stage 2 audit, within the agreed time-frame.

The stage 2 audit

Dates for the stage 2 audit were probably agreed and arranged by the auditor with the organization's management during the stage 1 audit. When the day arrives, the auditor – possibly with a team of auditors (dependent on the audit duration, and so on) – arrives to perform the actual audit of the implementation of the organization's Quality Management System.

Commencing with an opening meeting (described earlier), the auditor(s) will follow the defined plan, accommodating any unplanned adjustments as needed while still ensuring all the requirements are covered and that the organization's Quality Management System is fully assessed.

At the end of each audit day, it is typical for the results of the audit to be presented in a debriefing session. This gives an opportunity for any personnel who were not involved in the audit to hear what has been found, if anything, and to learn about what progress has been made and any deviations to the plan or changes for the next day(s). It is also an opportunity for the auditor(s) to indicate any potential audit trails that need to be followed to verify evidence found or to discuss the potential for any non-conformity to be mitigated based upon better explanation of the implementation evidence discovered.

At the end of the audit, the auditor(s) compiles a comprehensive report for submission to the certification body. The report is summarized at the closing meeting (defined earlier).

Although there is the possibility for one or more "major" non-conformities to be discovered during the stage 2 audit, the (lead) auditor will generally advise the organization's management as soon as it is found. Remember, a "major" non-conformity will prevent the auditor(s) from making recommendation for certification to be granted. Although the organization has the option to terminate the audit at this point, it is recommended to continue with the stage 2 audit for these reasons:

- the audit has been paid for, the certification body won't refund any audit time unused, and
- the audit should be completed as planned to reveal all existing issues, so they may be corrected.

Although during a stage 2 audit non-conformities may be discovered, a recommendation can be made by the auditor(s) for certification, if there are none of "major" significance (see previous section on grading of audit non-conformities).

The surveillance audit

On successful certification of an organization's Quality Management System, the organization moves into the "maintenance phase" of its certification. As defined in the registration agreement, the certification body is required to perform an audit at least annually. If sufficient time is required, a client may elect to have their surveillance audits conducted every six months, to the same total time.

The duration of the surveillance audit is defined in the IAF MD-5 document and is (typically) one-third (33%) of the duration of the stage 1 and stage 2 audits combined.

The surveillance audit is intended to focus on those aspects of the organization's Quality Management System that are closely related to the maintenance activities:

- any changes made to the Quality Management System
- management review(s) held since the previous audit
- internal audits conducted since the last audit
- corrective actions
- improvements
- customer feedback/complaints and
- previous audit non-conformities issued by the CB and associated actions

Over the two surveillance visits, the quality management will be sampled, in particular those aspects that are new and/or changed.

The surveillance audits also have opening and closing meetings and are reported in a similar manner to the certification audit. At the conclusion of the audit, the possible recommendation(s) relate to the ongoing certification or, in the case of significant audit non-conformities (see "major non-conformities"), the recommendation may be to undergo a "special visit" audit.

The triennial reassessment

On the third year after the date of the original certificate of certification was issued, a "triennial reassessment" is usually performed. Because the organization's Quality

Management System should be somewhat mature at this point, the certification body audit should focus on effectiveness or on corrective and improvement actions that have been taken over the previous years. With some three years of data available from customers' feedback, process performance, product conformity data, supplier evaluations, and so on, the organization's management should have a clear picture of the suitability of their Quality Management System as a tool to support growth.

As a result of employing a different focus during the triennial reassessment, the duration of this audit is less than the original certification audit. In fact, the MD-5 document allows the duration of the triennial reassessment to be two-thirds (66%) of the stage 1 and stage 2 audit durations combined.

On completion of a successful triennial reassessment, a recommendation may be made to issue a new certificate and the normal pattern of surveillance visits is implemented.

The "special visit" audit

There are circumstances under which an organization's certification body may require a "special visit" audit. The most significant event that leads to such an audit is when a "major" non-conformity is reported during the period of certification. As defined previously, a major non-conformity indicates that a failure in the Quality Management System has occurred. The nature of this type of systemic failure will usually require a significant corrective action to be undertaken by the organization and, rather than simply relying on records of the results, the certification body auditor may decide to carry out some on-site evaluation of the implementation that led to the records being produced.

Conducted in the manner described earlier, the auditor will focus on the (corrective) actions necessary to address the situation surrounding the major non-conformity. Additionally, the audit will also assess management review and internal audits as key indicators of the manner in which the corrective actions were managed.

At the conclusion of the special visit audit, one of three recommendations may be made and reported to the client, depending on the evidence presented by the client:

- The major non-conformity has been removed.
- Downgrading of the major to a minor non-conformity. Usually, a request will be made for further evidence of implementation of corrective actions to be provided at the next scheduled audit.
- Suspension of the organization's certificate of compliance. If a client hasn't taken (suitable) corrective actions to reduce the status of the major non-conformity, for whatever reason, the auditor is required to initiate suspension of the organization's certificate of compliance.

In addition to the preceding descriptions, it is always advisable to check with the particular certification body, to see how it handles the specifics of each type of audit service. In some circumstances, requirements are defined in a contractually binding agreement that forms the basis of its services to the client. Care should be taken to read any contract to ensure these provisions are well understood, as they often define specific responsibilities of the client.

CHAPTER 5: INTERNAL AUDITOR COMPETENCIES

For any internal management system audit program to be effective, it is of vital importance to have competent people managing, performing, and reporting them. ISO19011 goes into some depth of detail to list a number of attributes of auditors, which may, indeed, be desirable; however, in many internal audit programs, a number of key requirements for auditors are often overlooked.

"Never volunteer for anything"!

This famous saying, often attributed as coming from the military forces, should be taken at face value when considering who should perform internal management systems audits. There are many reasons why anyone who would volunteer, often when they have no practical experience of audits, shouldn't be selected without an evaluation of their competencies.

Apart from anything else, candidates for becoming internal auditors should be selected – or at least approved – by the management of the organization. It must not be overlooked that audits are a management tool and the credibility of the audit is of vital importance in determining the "health" of the management system.

ISO19011 section 7, includes many attributes that an auditor is supposed to possess. Often overlooked, however, are basic "blocking and tackling" like the abilities to communicate verbally and in writing as well as somewhat "advanced" skills such as critical-thinking abilities. The latter assists in the summation of facts that can lead to a conclusion being drawn, which should then be clearly – and concisely – reported to management.

It is not unusual for an auditor to be required to present their audit report to management. Typically, this involves reading the content of non-conformity statements and a summary of what they mean, often related to requirement of one or other of the ISO management standards. Techniques such as these are lifted directly from the auditor training courses, which themselves are based upon external audit behaviors, as discussed in earlier chapters.

If we employ the old adage, "It ain't what you say, it's the way that you say it," the underlying "message" of the audit reports can be lost in a dry, factual delivery style compounded by the technicalities of references to a Standard no one is that familiar with. Hardly surprising then, that anything which needs support from management to resolve can have its message, in effect, "lost." What's more, many audit reports are heard by the auditees in the same way as if they were being told they have ugly children!

Effective presentation skills can enhance the delivery of the "message" by carefully targeting those aspects that the audience (organization's management) should hear, so as to enlist their understanding and hence the need for action. The ability to summarize and present the "big picture" – including any risks – is improved when the presenter can speak clearly to an audience, preparing and employing the appropriate visual aids to communicate salient points.

ISO19011 defines some typical skills, knowledge, and education suitable for internal auditors for a number of specific ISO standards, for example, 9001, 14001, and 27001.

CHAPTER 6: USING THE RESULTS
OF INTERNAL AUDITS

If we are to consider much of the management process (required by the various ISO management system standards) as a network of interacting processes, it follows that the output of the internal audit process becomes an input to the management review of the system.

Since a management system internal audit is, by its nature, performed on the organization by its own personnel, there are four likely situations to report to management, within the associated requirement for the "management review." In the following scenarios, the internal audits are used as an independent "validation" for management, who are each reporting on the performance – to the stated objectives – of the process(es) for which they have responsibility.

PROCESS PERFORMANCE	INTERNAL AUDIT RESULTS	ACTIONS REQUIRED
Meets or exceeds targets set	QMS being followed (low/no risks)	Improvement of QMS?
Meets or exceeds targets set	QMS NOT being followed (what's the risk?)	Improve QMS in line with practice
Below targets set	QMS being followed (performance risk)	Corrective action required on process
Below targets set	QMS NOT being followed (risk analysis needed to determine actions)	Corrective action on QMS

If the required review of the management system is conducted not by a single, key member of the organization (often called the "management representative"), but by the various process owners reporting on their process, its objectives, and current performance, the results of the audits can be used to focus on any need for action – and also provides the independent validation desired – the fundamental purpose of performing internal audits.

A comprehensive review by management will also provide an excellent opportunity to direct the focus of the coming internal audits, once again, to address those aspects that may present:

"An undesirable situation or circumstance that has both a likelihood of occurring and a potentially negative consequence" or the "effect of uncertainty on objectives."

CHAPTER 7: RISK BASED INTERNAL AUDIT CASE STUDIES

The following case studies give examples where an internal audit was focused on ensuring resolution of a situation that put the organization at risk, by focusing not simply on compliance to documents, but by looking to process performance, cause/effect, and the "sequence and interactions" of the processes of a management system.

CASE STUDY #1

An internal audit was conducted in a large and well-established manufacturer of industrial machinery. The organization had been certified to ISO9001 since the early 1990s. The focus of the audit was the processing of product non-conformity reports in the metal parts fabrication department. This department made sheet metal parts, such as guards for moving parts, heat shields, pipe work, and similar components.

The audit began by looking at the (large) number of pallets in the non-conforming area of the inspection bay. A quick check of the copies of the non-conformance reports, written by the inspectors, revealed that the main reason was the parts were not to the engineering drawings, being dimensionally incorrect – usually the dimensions were larger on the radii of bends, lengths, or similar characteristics.

These parts were awaiting disposition, which usually meant a quality engineer would review the nature of the non-conformances and liaise with personnel who work in the next process in the production cycle, the assembly shop where the components are brought together, prior to functional test. The vast majority of parts were, indeed, totally acceptable for use (fit, form, and function were unaffected) and the assembly personnel confirmed these parts were no different to the previous rejects that had also been accepted for use. The quality engineer, having confirmed acceptability, then initiated the paperwork to approve the use of the non-conforming product with the disposition of "use as is." While all this activity was going on, Production Control had to flag the components being on shortage, which halted production in the assembly area.

Each product non-conformity occurrence was entered into a database that had been created by the organization's own Information Technology department. The auditor asked to see an analysis of the various non-conformities and was shown that the database had no functionality when it came to analysis of the database – so no reporting was possible. The auditor spent some time reviewing the database and discovered nearly 8,000 entries over the course of a year.

Since no reports were available to dispute the costs, the auditor estimated that the total amount of money the organization was expending in the whole process of dealing with the non-conforming parts was close to $8M ($1,000/occurrence). Furthermore, the assembly department had their own reporting methods, including key failure categories found by the last process – final test.

These were:

- missing parts
- loose parts
- foreign objects/debris

The costs associated with the subsequent teardown and repair of the product was also entered into the same database, but without any ability to analyze why. The reporting observed by the internal auditor was in the form of a set of charts prepared on a PC in the Assembly Department main office and posted on the office windows. As a result of the need for teardown and repair of the finished product, the actual costs associated with the whole story were actually much higher than the $8M estimated.

With this information, the auditor reported to the president of the organization that a substantial saving had been identified, in the preceding amount – and didn't mention any "ISO" requirement, clause numbers, or paraphrased any text from the Standard.

The president was immediately excited to hear this, since $8M was approximately equal to six months of sales revenue! Quite a sizable risk!

Needless to say, the president put his full weight behind the organization's resolution of the problems, including the fact that the IT department should escalate the database reporting function from #13 on its list of priorities…

CASE STUDY #2

The following is an account of how an internal audit leads to the removal of a major source of risk through the identification of the cause of a 60% rework loop in the production cycle. This rework was generally carried out on the "off shift" at premium pay rates, over the normal 8–5 day rate of pay.

The organization performed four processes on client documentation:

- photocopying
- document categorization/sorting
- digital imaging
- database loading

During the initial internal audits of the processes, in preparation for the third-party certification audit, each process was audited and, during the audit of the digital imaging process, it was discovered that nearly 60% of the imaged work is rejected and has to be "reworked." The auditor asked what caused the problem and the supervisor described the situation:

Each job being imaged has to be checked 100% for completeness – in this case each digital "page" must be EXACTLY the same as the original, meaning no blank areas, cut-off text, incomplete information and so on.

During processing it was discovered that, in some cases, there were blank pages where there should have been a page with a simple word printed on it. Although these documents could be thousands of pages, a single unwanted blank page would cause the total quantity to be reprocessed –

it could indicate several pages skipped through the automated scanner without being imaged correctly, if at all.

By discussions with the process operators and tracing back through the process, it was discovered that the blank page was caused not by a blank page, but by a single page stamped with a single word. This unique, stamped page is used as a "placeholder" within the document, to indicate to the reader they should review a related document – often in another medium (tape, film etc.). Through interviewing the person responsible for stamping the single sheet of paper and inserting it into the document to be scanned, it was discovered the inking pad would dry out, and not transfer sufficient ink to produce a complete, black impression, and that in turn, although the word was visible to the naked, human eye, it didn't possess sufficient carbon (which the document scanner detects) to create an image.

As a direct result of identifying the nature of the process problem, the organization's management called a cross-functional team together to work on an improvement and the issue was resolved overnight.

ANNEX 1: COMPARISON OF REQUIREMENTS FOR INTERNAL AUDITS

Throughout the various standards for management systems, one of the common themes is that of internal audits. Since the ISO9001 Standard for quality management systems pre-dates most other management systems standards, it can be seen that the ISO9001 Standard was used as the model for the internal audit requirements in a substantial manner. The requirements are either used almost verbatim (ASIS SPC.1) or employ significantly similar phrases or concepts.

The following table includes the various internal audit requirements extracted from their parent Standard.

ISO9001:2008 QUALITY MANAGEMENT SYSTEMS – REQUIREMENTS	8.2.2	The organization shall conduct internal audits at planned intervals to determine whether the quality management system.
		a) conforms to the planned arrangements (see 7.1), to the requirement of this International Standard and to the quality management system requirements established by the organization, and
		b) is effectively implemented and maintained.

An audit programme shall be planned, taking into consideration the status and importance of the processes and areas to be audited, as well as the results of previous audits. The audit criteria, scope, frequency and methods shall be defined. The selection of auditors and conduct of audits shall ensure objectivity and impartiality of the audit process. Auditors shall not audit their own work.

A documented procedure shall be established to define the responsibilities and requirements for planning and conducting audits, establishing records and reporting results.

Records of the audits and their results shall be maintained (see 4.2.4).

The management responsible for the area being audited shall ensure that any necessary corrections and corrective actions are taken without undue delay to eliminate detected nonconformities and their causes.

ISO13485:2003

MEDICAL DEVICES –
QUALITY MANAGEMENT SYSTEMS –
REQUIREMENTS FOR REGULATORY PURPOSES

8.2.2 The organization shall conduct internal audits at planned intervals to determine whether the quality management system.

a) conforms to the planned arrangements (see 7.1), to the requirement of this International Standard and to the quality management system requirements established by the organization, and

b) is effectively implemented and maintained.

An audit programme shall be planned, taking into consideration the status and importance of the processes and areas to be audited, as well as the results of previous audits. The audit criteria, scope, frequency and methods shall be defined. The selection of auditors and conduct of audits shall ensure objectivity and impartiality of the audit process. Auditors shall not audit their own work.

A documented procedure shall be established to define the responsibilities and requirements for planning and conducting audits, establishing records and reporting results.

Records of the audits and their results shall be maintained (see 4.2.4).

The management responsible for the area being audited shall ensure that any necessary corrections and corrective actions are taken without undue delay to eliminate detected nonconformities and their causes.

ISO14001:2004 **ENVIRONMENTAL MANAGEMENT SYSTEMS – REQUIREMENTS**	4.5.5	The organization shall ensure that internal audits of the environmental management system are conducted at planned intervals to: a) 1) conforms to planned arrangements for environmental management including the requirements of

this international standard, and

2) has been properly implemented and is maintained, and

b) provide information on the results of audits to management

Audit programme(s) shall be planned, established, implemented and maintained by the organization, taking into consideration the environmental importance of the operation(s) concerned and the results of previous audits.

Audit procedure(s) shall be established, implemented and maintained that address

- The responsibilities and requirements for planning and conducting audits, reporting results and retaining associated records.

- The determination of audit criteria, scope, frequency and methods.

Selection of auditors and conduct of audits shall ensure objectivity and impartiality of the audit process.

ISO20000-1:2011

INFORMATION TECHNOLOGY – SERVICE MANAGEMENT PT 1 SERVICE MANAGEMENT SYSTEM REQUIREMENTS

The service provider shall conduct internal audits, at planned intervals, to determine whether the SMS and the services:

a) fulfill the requirements of this part of ISO/IEC 20000;

b) fulfill the service requirements and the SMS requirements identified by the service provider;

c) are effectively implemented and maintained.

There shall be a documented procedure including the authorities and responsibilities for planning and conducting audits, reporting audit results and maintaining audit records.

An audit programme shall be planned. This shall take into consideration the status and importance of the processes and areas to be audited, as well as the results of previous audits. The audit criteria, scope, frequency and methods shall be documented.

The selection of auditors and conduct of audits shall ensure objectivity and impartiality of the audit. Auditors shall not audit their own work.

Nonconformities shall be communicated, prioritized and responsibility allocated for actions. The management responsible for the area being audited shall ensure that any corrections and corrective actions are taken without undue delay to eliminate nonconformities and their causes. Follow-up activities shall include verification of the actions taken and the reporting of results.

ISO27001:2013

INFORMATION TECHNOLOGY – SECURITY TECHNIQUES – INFORMATION SECURITY MANAGEMENT SYSTEMS – REQUIREMENTS

9.2   The organization shall conduct internal audits at planned intervals to provide information on whether the information security management system:

a) conforms to

1) the organization's own requirements for its information security management system; and

2) the requirements of this International Standard;

b) is effectively implemented and maintained.

The organization shall:

c) plan, establish, implement and maintain an audit programme(s), including the frequency, methods, responsibilities, planning requirements and reporting. The audit programme(s) shall take into consideration the importance of the processes concerned and the results of previous audits;

d) define the audit criteria and scope for each audit;

e) select auditors and conduct audits that ensure objectivity and the impartiality of the audit process;

f) ensure that the results of the audits are reported to relevant management; and

g) retain documented information as evidence of the audit programme(s) and the audit results.

ASIS SPC.1 **ORGANIZATIONAL RESILIENCE STANDARD**	4.5.5	The organization shall conduct OR management system audits at planned intervals, and from time to time on a periodic basis (as determined by the management of the organization) to determine whether the control objectives, controls, processes, and procedures of its OR management system:

a) conform to the requirements of this standard and relevant legislation or regulations;

b) Conform to the organization's risk management requirements;

c) Are effectively implemented and maintained, and;

d) Perform as expected

An audit program shall be planned, taking into consideration the status and importance of the processes and areas to be audited, as well as the results of previous audits. The audit criteria, scope and frequency, and methods shall be defined. The selection of auditors and conduct of audits shall ensure objectivity and impartiality of the audit process. Auditors shall not audit their own work.

The responsibilities and requirements for planning and conducting audits, and for reporting results and maintaining records (see 4.5.4) shall be defined in a documented procedure.

The management responsible for the area being audited shall ensure that actions are taken without undue delay to eliminate detected nonconformities and their causes. Follow-up activities shall include the verification of the actions taken and the reporting of verification results.

ISO/IEC 17021:2011

CONFORMITY ASSESSMENT – REQUIREMENTS FOR BODIES PROVIDING AUDIT AND CERTIFICATION OF MANAGEMENT SYSTEMS

10.3.6 Internal audits (If option of compliance to ISO9001 not used).

10.3.6.1 The certification body shall establish procedures for internal audits to verify that it fulfils the requirements of this International Standard and that the management system is effectively implemented and maintained.

NOTE ISO19011 provides guidelines for conducting internal audits.

10.3.6.2 An audit programme shall be planned, taking into consideration the importance of the processes and areas to be audited, as well as the results of previous audits.

10.3.6.3 Internal audits shall be performed at least once

every 12 months. The frequency of internal audits may be reduced if the certification body can demonstrate that its management system continues to be effectively implemented according to this International Standard and has proven stability.

10.3.6.4 The certification body shall ensure that

a) internal audits are conducted by qualified personnel knowledgeable in certification, auditing and the requirements of this International Standard,

b) auditors do not audit their own work,

c) personnel responsible for the area audited are informed of the outcome of the audit, d) any actions resulting from internal audits are taken in a timely and appropriate manner, and

e) any opportunities for improvement are identified.

ISO22301:2012   9.2   The organization shall conduct internal audits at planned intervals to provide information on:

whether the business continuity management system

a) conforms to

     1)   the organization's own requirements for its BCMS,

     2)   the requirements of this International Standard

b) is effectively implemented and maintained.

The organization shall

- plan, establish, implement and maintain (an) audit programme(s), including the frequency, methods, responsibilities, planning requirements and reporting. The audit programme(s) shall take into consideration the importance of the processes concerned and the results of previous audits.

- select auditors and conduct audits to ensure objectivity and the impartiality of the audit process,

- ensure that the results of the audits are reported to relevant management, and

- retain documented information as evidence of the implementation of the audit programme and the audit results.

The audit programme, including any schedule, shall be based on the results of the risk assessments of the organization's activities, and the results of previous audits. The audit procedures shall cover the scope, frequency, methodologies and competencies, as well as the responsibilities and requirements for conducting audits and reporting results.

The management responsible for the are being audited shall ensure that any necessary corrections and corrective actions are taken without undue delay to eliminate detected nonconformities and their causes.

Follow-up activities shall include the verification of the actions taken and the reporting of verification results.

APPENDIX 1: THE FOOTBALL© PLANNING TOOL

In the section on audit planning, the creation of checklists and so on by the auditor was discussed. There are significant merits to the individual preparation for an audit by the assigned auditor. Rather than develop (or use an already developed set of) questions to ask, checklists need only be those things that the auditor will use to begin a discussion – much as a shopping list is used by someone on a grocery shopping trip. Only simple prompts are really necessary to have a conversation with the various people who manage or operate a process.

As with other forms of interview, it is of value to know what answers should be given to a specific question. If, during an audit, an individual is asked about the availability of a particular form, used to record vital data on product or service measurement, it is important for the auditor to know what the answer "should" be, based on what the management system defines. If the "Football" diagram is created as a form and is populated, by the auditor, with these "answers" – or at least the appropriate responses that should be given – the auditor has a number of advantages.

The act of studying the various criteria from the defined management system documentation (manual, process maps, procedures, instructions etc.) means the auditor should develop a much higher level of comprehension of the various supporting processes and controls, which will lead to a more effective audit.

If included on the diagram, from the auditor planning/preparation task, the specific details that are identified to be a risk contributor, the auditor will be sure to go into the audit able to hold a meaningful discussion.

The auditor may use the diagram to construct the key information needed to verify the management system is being practiced as planned (the so-called "planned arrangements").

Practice shows that the same document (on which the Football© is printed) may also be used to record the auditors notes, which makes the process much more efficient.

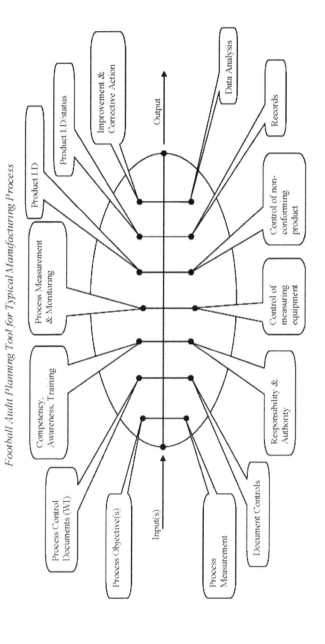

Football Audit Planning Tool for Typical Manufacturing Process

Product I.D

Product I.D/status

Improvement & Corrective Action

Data Analysis

Records

Output

Control of non-conforming product

Process Measurement & Monitoring

Control of measuring equipment

Competency, Awareness, Training

Responsibility & Authority

Process Control Documents (WI)

Process Objective(s)

Input(s)

Process Measurement

Document Controls

ITG RESOURCES

IT Governance Ltd sources, creates and delivers products and services to meet the real-world, evolving IT governance needs of today's organisations, directors, managers and practitioners.

The ITG website (*www.itgovernance.co.uk*) is the international one-stop-shop for corporate and IT governance information, advice, guidance, books, tools, training and consultancy. On the website you will find the following pages related to the subject matter of this book:

www.itgovernance.co.uk/it_audit.aspx

www.itgovernance.co.uk/standards.aspx

www.itgovernance.co.uk/iso9001-quality-management-standards.aspx

www.itgovernance.co.uk/iso31000.aspx.

Publishing Services

IT Governance Publishing (ITGP) is the world's leading IT-GRC publishing imprint that is wholly owned by IT Governance Ltd.

With books and tools covering all IT governance, risk and compliance frameworks, we are the publisher of choice for authors and distributors alike, producing unique and practical publications of the highest quality, in the latest formats available, which readers will find invaluable.

www.itgovernancepublishing.co.uk is the website dedicated to ITGP. Other titles published by ITGP that may be of interest include:

- Exploding the Myths Surrounding ISO9000

  www.itgovernance.co.uk/shop/p-1292.aspx

- Swanson on Internal Auditing

  www.itgovernance.co.uk/shop/p-1142.aspx

- IT Strategic and Operational Controls

  www.itgovernance.co.uk/shop/p-789.aspx.

We also offer a range of off-the-shelf toolkits *t*hat give comprehensive, customisable documents to help users create the specific documentation they need to properly implement a management system or standard. Written by experienced practitioners and based on the latest best practice, ITGP toolkits can save months of work for organisations working towards compliance with a given standard.

Toolkits that may be of interest include:

- ISO9001 QMS Quality Management System Documentation Toolkit

  www.itgovernance.co.uk/shop/p-1259.aspx

- ISO14001 EMS Environmental Management System Documentation Toolkit

  www.itgovernance.co.uk/shop/p-1247.aspx

- ISO/IEC 20000 Documentation Toolkit

  www.itgovernance.co.uk/shop/p-632.aspx.

Books and tools published by IT Governance Publishing (ITGP) are available from all business booksellers and the following websites:

www.itgovernance.eu   *www.itgovernanceusa.com*

www.itgovernance.in   *www.itgovernancesa.co.za*

www.itgovernance.asia.

Training Services

IT Governance offers an extensive portfolio of training courses designed to educate information security, IT governance, risk management and compliance professionals. Our classroom and online training programmes will help you develop the skills required to deliver best practice and compliance to your organisation. They will also enhance your career by providing you with industry standard certifications and increased peer recognition. Our range of courses offer a structured learning path from Foundation to Advanced level in the key topics of Information Security, IT governance, Business Continuity and Service Management.

Full details of all IT Governance training courses can be found at *www.itgovernance.co.uk/training.aspx*.

Professional Services and Consultancy

IT Governance consultants have many years of experience supporting internal audits and providing supplier audits (part of supply chain auditing and supply chain assurance) for quality-conscious organisations that want to ensure they have put in place/comply with the requirements of management systems for:

- Quality management systems (e.g. ISO9001)
- Information security (e.g. ISO/IEC 27001)
- Business continuity (e.g. ISO22301)
- Environmental management systems (e.g. ISO14001)
- Health and Safety management systems (e.g. OHSAH18001).

We can help you to improve the management of all your internal processes, focusing on quality areas that positively affect your ability to win orders and deliver what your customers require, consistently, on time and at a profitable, yet economic price. Part of this cost-effective service includes showing you how to obtain top management support in key areas such as:

- Audit planning
- Auditor selection/competency
- Post audit actions

By using our tried and trusted knowledge transfer approach, you will see a rapid drop in the level of non-conformances to specified requirements that will quickly allow you to achieve accredited certification to a number of international standards.

For more information about IT Governance Consultancy services, see: *www.itgovernance.co.uk/consulting.aspx*.

Newsletter

IT governance is one of the hottest topics in business today, not least because it is also the fastest moving.

You can stay up to date with the latest developments across the whole spectrum of IT governance subject matter, including; risk management, information security, ITIL and IT service management, project governance, compliance and so much more, by subscribing to ITG's core publications and topic alert emails.

Simply visit our subscription centre and select your preferences: *www.itgovernance.co.uk/newsletter.aspx*.

EU for product safety is Stephen Evans, The Mill Enterprise Hub, Stagreenan, Drogheda, Co. Louth, A92 CD3D, Ireland. (servicecentre@itgovernance.eu)

www.ingramcontent.com/pod-product-compliance
Lightning Source LLC
Chambersburg PA
CBHW070835070326
40690CB00009B/1552